You're Hired!

SECRETS TO SUCCESSFUL JOB INTERVIEWS

Sharon McDonnell

Macmillan • USA

Second Edition

The before and after résumés on pp 28-31 are reprinted from
"Through the Brick Wall: Resumé Builder"
by Kate Wendleton (Five O'Clock Books).
Reprinted with permission of author.
All rights reserved.

Macmillan General Reference
A Simon & Schuster Macmillan Company
1633 Broadway
New York, NY 10019

Library of Congress Number: 97-81091

ISBN: 0-02-862510-2

Manufactured in the United States of America
10   9   8   7   6   5   4   3   2   1

CONTENTS

ACKNOWLEDGMENTS

A debt of gratitude is owed to numerous people who kindly lent their time and expertise to help in the writing of this book. Very special thanks to employment law journalist Phillip M Perry, who contributed to the chapter on illegal questions, and to Kate Wendleton of The Five O'Clock Club and Ruth K. Robbins of Résumés Plus, who contributed résumés.

Warm thank-yous to executive recruiters Dale Winston and Richard Linde of Battalia Winston International; Bill Heyman and Elisabeth Ryan of Heyman Associates; Barbara Barra of outplacement firm Lee Hecht Harrison; résumé and job counseling expert Stanley Wynett and career development expert Nancy Josephs of Brookshire Enterprises. Dr. Paul J. Rosch of the American Institute of Stress was very helpful on how job-seekers can combat stress. Virginia Sullivan of Image Communications International and executive development consultant Carolyn Mann deserve thanks for advice on how to dress and act at interviews.

A round of applause to the corporate interviewers who donated their views from the other side of the desk: Pat Galloway of William Morris; Michele Glasser of Microsoft; Dwight W. Tierney of Viacom; Brent C. Inman of Coopers & Lybrand; Maria Fornario of Burson-Marsteller; Daniel J. Fanok of Colgate-Palmolive; James Hagy of Jones Day Reavis Pogue; Kevin Bergin of Grey Advertising; Chuck Dombeck of Pfizer; Colette Gardner of Bankers Trust; and Kenneth Feldman of Hearst Magazines.

I am very grateful to my editors, Ellen Lichtenstein and Linda Bernbach, who offered many excellent suggestions and changes on my manuscript.

CHAPTER ONE

Job Search Techniques

As the security of lifelong employment with one company rapidly disappears due to downsizings, mergers, and thousands of layoffs, today's average worker can expect to hold eight jobs in a lifetime. Survival demands that job-seekers develop a highly focused, organized, and comprehensive approach to the job hunt.

Methods that have worked just fine in the past such as combing the classified ads or haunting employment agencies—or even a scattershot approach—can no longer be counted upon. Job-seekers must apply ingenuity and creativity to the job search following job leads from sources as diverse as networking—through which an estimated 80 percent of all jobs are filled—to research to trade associations. Applicants should cast a net as wide as possible, encompassing not only large corporations, but small businesses—where most of the growth in U.S. business is—nonprofit organizations, and so on in order to reel in as many potential job interviews as they can.

A job search plan with the greatest chances for success in penetrating the "hidden" job market—where most job leads lie—should feature as many of the following techniques as possible.

CLASSIFIED ADS

Responding to classified ads is a helpful part of your job hunt. But please don't make the serious mistake of thinking it's the be-all and end-all. Collective wisdom on answering ads can be distilled into a few words: read them carefully; answer a lot of them; don't expect much.

The odds are against you. Most job openings never even hit the newspapers. Only an estimated 15% of all job openings are advertised. In addition, a good ad in a major newspaper can result in several thousand résumés. In most cases, résumés are screened by someone other than the hiring manager.

Reading ads is enlightening in the sense that it gives you an idea of which companies in your industry are hiring, the backgrounds and skills they are seeking, the salaries they are willing to pay, and the executive recruiting firms they are dealing with. Scan major daily newspapers in your area, such as *The New York Times* or *Miami Herald*. Sunday is usually the day when the classified section runs, but don't forget to check sections, such as the business section, for additional job leads. Trade publications are an even better bet than newspapers, since their ads target a specific industry. Also consult national newspapers, such as the *Wall Street Journal* and the *National Business Employment Weekly*, both published by Dow Jones. NBEW lists ads culled from regional editions of the *Wall Street Journal*.

Don't forget to look under several headings for jobs. For example, positions requiring writing can be found under "Editorial," "Writer," "Technical Writer," "Proposal Writer," "Public Relations," "Copywriting," "Publishing," "Advertising," and "Communications." Marketing manager positions can be found under the specific industry they are in or under the general heading "Marketing."

It's a good idea to scan back issues of newspapers. Some advertised positions may still be open—or the employee hired may now be gone. Résumés are often kept much longer than you may think. I once obtained a part-time university teaching position for a media writing workshop *one year* after I answered the ad in *The New York Times*.

RESEARCH

Research is a far better method for locating job leads than reading the classifieds. Through research you can uncover information about your industry that can help you to impress interviewers, to sell yourself with a more targeted résumé and cover letter, and to locate networking contacts. Information is power, the expression goes, and in today's lean, mean, and competitive market, it is more essential than ever to distinguish yourself from other applicants.

Comprehensive research can answer questions in the following three areas:

Industry Information

- What are the trends in this field?
- What are the growth areas?
- Which companies are the major players in this field?
- What are the major challenges and problems in this field?

Company Information

- What are its weak points?
- What are its strong points?
- How is the company organized?
- Which companies are major competitors?
- What is the company culture like?

Job Information

- What are the tasks and responsibilities?
- What are typical salaries?
- Who should be contacted for openings?
- What are the qualifications for people hired for this job?
- Is the company in a hiring mode at present?

Start your research at a library with an extensive business reference section. Librarians can save you loads of time and can be very helpful; don't hesitate to tell them what you are looking for. Compile a list of companies in your chosen industry and geographic area for a direct mail campaign. Obtain company addresses, telephone numbers, and names of executives. Locate articles containing "insider" information on companies that interest you and on industry trends in newspapers and general business and trade publications.

Trade publications, which report on specific industries in great depth, can be very valuable. Articles that profile different companies, offer industry round-ups, describe trends, or are written by industry experts can clue you in to the "hidden" job market. For example, companies expanding to different cities, opening new divisions, or marketing hot new products will most likely be hiring. Columns listing new clients and new businesses can offer job leads. So can "executive changes" and "people in the news" columns, which can keep you informed of who's who in an industry, offer potential networking contacts, and alert you to personnel changes and possible job openings. "Events" and "weeks ahead" columns can tell you about upcoming meetings, seminars, and conventions held by trade associations. "Help wanted" ads will offer many job openings not mentioned in newspapers and can be scanned for salary ranges for different positions, as well. Special annual or semiannual issues that numerically rank the top companies in an industry are also useful.

Reference sources that are helpful include:

- Directories
- Periodical Indexes
- Trade Publications
- Annual Reports and Brochures

Directories

Directories in Print or *Guide to American Directories*—Listings of thousands of directories, both general business and specific industries.

Standard & Poor's Register of Corporations, Directors and Executives—Listings of thousands of U.S. corporations with names and titles of top officers.

Moody's Industrial Manual—Listings of thousands of public companies as well as international companies.

Dun's Million Dollar Directory—Listings of thousands of businesses in many industries, such as industrial, banking/finance, utilities with names and titles of top officers.

Encyclopedia of Business Information Sources—Listings of magazines, newsletters, and handbooks on business topics.

Gale Directory of Publications—Listings of newspapers, magazines, and trade publications.

Standard Rate and Data Service: Business Publication Rates and Data—Listings of business and trade publications.

Standard Periodical Directory—Listings of thousands of magazines, newsletters, and directories.

(For directories on specific industries, consult the Appendix.)

Periodical Indexes

Business Periodicals Index—Listings of hundreds of magazines, including top trade publications.

The New York Times Index—Indexes of all issues.

Wall Street Journal Index—Monthly index of all issues.

Predicasts F&S Index United States—Indexes and abstracts of newspapers, business and trade publications, and government reports in detail.

National General Business Publications

Fortune

Business Week

Forbes

Inc.

Barron's

Local General Business Publications

Crain's New York Business (editions also for Chicago, Cleveland, Detroit)

California Business

New Jersey Business

Trade Publications

Advertising Age

Electronic Media

Real Estate Forum

American Banker

Computerworld

Women's Wear Daily

Automotive News

(For trade publications of specific industries, see the Appendix.)

National Newspapers

The New York Times

Los Angeles Times

Wall Street Journal

National Business Employment Weekly

ANNUAL REPORTS AND BROCHURES

Annual reports and brochures can offer a great deal of useful information about a company, from financial data to how different divisions are doing to new product development. Just remember, though, to read between the lines; they must be read without the rose-colored vision of the public relations department that issues them. Due to federal disclosure requirements, the figures in annual reports are accurate and can reveal trends in sales and the ratio between revenues and profits, but understanding annual reports requires some knowledge of basic finance Read recruitment brochures for details on training programs, recruiting methods, and employment policies.

PROFESSIONAL AND TRADE ORGANIZATIONS

Professional and trade associations are a goldmine of contacts, information, and potential opportunities, and a great way to tap into the "hidden" job market. You should join at least one in your field. It is best to become active and view membership as a long-term career strategy, so that you have an existing network of contacts and resources when you're looking for a job. Attend meetings and seminars of your local chapter regularly to meet members and be briefed on trends and issues pertaining to your field, as well as the annual convention, if one is held. Belong to or chair a committee—such as events, publicity, or membership—since this is an especially good way to develop a higher profile in your industry.

The Encyclopedia of Associations, found in most libraries, lists over 20,000 associations alphabetically by industry, as well as contact names, addresses, and telephone numbers. These range widely from the Public Relations Society of America, Institute of Electrical and Electronics Engineers, American Marketing Association, Academy of TV Arts and Sciences to the National Retail Merchants Association. Some are for women only, such as the National Association for Female Executives and American Women in Radio and Television, or for minorities, such as the National Association of Black Accountants.

All associations have membership directories, which can be invaluable for a telephone or direct-mail job search. Most publish newsletters, which offer members opportunities to author articles on relevant topics to become better known. Many also publish trade magazines, which run lengthy articles on industry trends, e.g., which companies are expanding or downsizing, etc., and also welcome articles by professionals in the field. Trade magazines run classified ads, which are mostly for higher-level positions not advertised in newspapers, and announcement of appointments or promotions to new positions. Some trade associations also have extensive libraries, literature, and research sources that can further your job hunt.

NETWORKING

Networking means plumbing all the professional and social contacts you have for information and referrals to help you get a job. Most people have no idea how many people they really know, nor the treasure trove these contacts can be. A common job-hunting mistake is to expect close friends to provide the best help in finding a job. Very often, this is not the case—with the most valuable leads generated by casual acquaintances or even a stranger met for the first time. One psychologist recalls she obtained several speaking engagements through her seatmate on an airplane ride, a business owner with whom she kept in contact by mail.

Experts say contacts are people who will take your call and remember you. So start talking to practically everyone about your search for a job—you never know.

Everyone belongs to many different networks. Some of these include:

- colleagues in your current workplace
- ex-colleagues from your former workplaces
- friends, acquaintances, neighbors
- professional affiliations
- family
- volunteer work
- non-work groups (sports, social, educational, etc.)
- religious affiliations
- school friends
- clients
- suppliers of professional services (lawyers, accountants, bankers)

Networks should be built and nurtured carefully over time. While you can call or write people you have not talked to for years, you should ideally touch base with your contacts a couple of times a year to exchange news and pleasantries. One method many people use with professional colleagues is to send articles of interest with a "FYI" note attached.

Career expert Emily Koltnow, co-author of *Congratulations! You've Been Fired*, lectures on "how to meet 1,800 people at lunch." (That's a lunch with seven people.) What she means is: "The average number of contacts that someone knows is 250. Some know many more. Whenever you meet someone, you're talking to everyone they know." Because of this multiplier effect—and the fact that you never know the potential value of a person's contacts—"you do yourself a disservice if you say you're fine when you're really looking for a job."

Networking is a delicate art with its own etiquette. You should remain gracious and professional at all times, and not cross the fine line between being tenacious and being pushy. It's best not to ask any of your contacts bluntly for a job. A better approach is to ask for information about the industry or a specific company and for names of people to talk to. The key is to build a chain of referrals that will eventually lead to a job opening for which you are well-suited. It's also best not to give your résumé out when you start networking—it may shut you out of potential jobs—but to tailor it to specific job openings. You should network in an organized, efficient fashion by keeping track of names, telephone numbers, key facts, dates seen, referral names, etc., in a notebook or computer. This file should be updated periodically, even after you obtain a new job.

When you call referrals, quickly introduce yourself, mention the name of the contact who referred you, and ask for a meeting to discuss the industry or company in question or a convenient time to talk if a meeting is not possible. Listen and ask intelligent questions based on your research about the industry or company during the meeting. Again, don't ask for a job. Send a personalized thank you note soon after the meeting, so you will be remembered. The note should emphasize skills you have that are relevant to the job you are seeking, or perhaps recall a noteworthy remark made by the referral. You can contact your referrals periodically to inform them of your progress in following advice or calling other referrals they have made, since you want to continue old contacts as well as build new ones.

Don't overlook formal networking groups. *The National Business Employment Weekly* lists event calendars of job search and support groups by state, ranging from Forty Plus to The Five O'Clock Club to classes at colleges and churches. Women's networks across the country are listed in the membership directory of the National Association for Female Executives or can be located by calling 800-634-NAFE.

ELECTRONIC DATABASES

This is the way to truly bring your job search into the 21st century. You can scan thousands of job listings, acquire lists of companies in your targeted industries, obtain news articles and financial data on these companies, and post your résumé to potential employers by using a computer connected to the Internet or a commercial online service, such as America Online or Compuserve. You can also browse newspaper classifieds more easily online than you can in print; just type in relevant keywords, and presto, all the ads containing these words will pop up on your screen. Since many newspapers post their ads online before they appear in print, you can get a headstart on the competition by researching online. And if you're thinking about relocating, you can check the classified sections of out-of-town newspapers online to get an idea of what the job market is like in areas you are considering.

The wealth of information that can be at your fingertips within seconds by going online will astonish you. Employers are also finding that they can get fast responses from a national audience by posting jobs online. Even if you don't have a computer, a modem and an Internet provider, you don't have to miss out on this extremely valuable resource. Many public and university libraries allow walk-in use of their Internet-connected computers. Computer centers, Internet cafes and Kinko's copy shops also rent Internet computer time by the hour.

INTERNET JOB BANKS

There are huge job banks on the Internet, where you can search thousands of job listings by occupation, job title or state. Career Mosaic (*www.careermosaic.com*) for example, has over 70,000 job listings worldwide, including many in accounting, finance, health care, insurance and electrical engineering as well as computer-related job areas. There's even a special section for recent college graduates. You can add your résumé to the database of over 50,000 résumés employers can browse. Thanks to a partnership with The Five O"Clock Club, Career Mosaic also offers articles on the club's job hunting strategies and a coaching section, which allows you to e-mail your job-hunting questions to a career coach. Monster Board (*www. monster.com*), which lists over 50,000 jobs, will send likely job listings to you by e-mail after you complete a profile of the type of job you are seeking. Trade shows and job fairs are also listed at Monster Board, and you can post your résumé there as well.

E-Span (*www.espan.com*) lists thousands of jobs in almost every industry from education, sales and finance to medicine.It includes a résumé database and will regularly e-mail appropriate listings to you. An extensive career counseling section provides career outlook and salary survey information from the *Occupational Outlook Handbook* together with articles from experts on creating résumés and interviewing. At Career Path (*www.careerpath.com*) you can find help wanted ads from dozens of newspapers nationwide along with job listings from many company sites. At Online Career Center (*www.occ.com*) you can post your résumé and browse through job listings in such areas as hospitality, retail, nursing and sales. In addition to these general job banks, there are also specialized job banks for particular industries including:

- MedSearch (*www.medsearch.com*) for health care
- FedWorld (*www.fedworld.gov*) for Federal government jobs
- Nonprofit Career Network (*www.nonprofitcareer.com*) for jobs in the nonprofit sector

Some of these job banks, such as E-Span and Online Career Center, are also found on commercial online services. America Online has a Careers section and Compuserve a Career Management Forum, where you can take part in online 'chats' with experts, exchange leads with others on bulletin boards, and read job-related articles posted to their electronic libraries.

Professional and managerial job listings, articles from the *Wall Street Journal* and *National Business Employment Weekly*, and salary surveys can be found at Wall Steet Journal Interactive's Careers (*http://careers.wsj.com*).

For college students and alumni, JOBTRAK (*www.jobtrak,com*) lists jobs from over 750 college career centers and offers a résumé database and salary calculators for the cost of living in different cities. ProNet provides a job listing service for the alumni of 20 colleges (mainly Ivy League and other select state and private schools such as the University of Michigan and UCLA). Call your alumni association to see if it uses ProNet. If so, you will be directed to the specific school site. There's a $50 fee for using ProNet.

The number of companies that post available jobs on their Web sites is growing rapidly. Currently these include Aetna, American Airlines, Blockbuster, Walt Disney Co., Toys 'R Us, Wells Fargo, United Nations, and AT&T to name just a few. Many trade associations also post job listings on their Web sites as a service to members. Members of the American Marketing Association, the American Medical Association, the Graphic Artists Guild and the Physical Therapy Association can start their job search on the Net. Many college alumni associations also post job listings on the net. You can check the list at College/University Homepages (*www.mit.edu.8001/people/cdemello/univ.html*) to see if your college is included.

RESEARCHING COMPANIES ONLINE

Researching companies on the Internet is a cinch. Hoover's Online (*www.hoovers,com*) offers free much of the information published in its company directories, including company profiles, addresses and telephone numbers, annual sales, top executives and job openings. You can search by name of company, industry, amount of sales, or region. Dun & Bradstreet (*www.dnb.com*) offers business background reports including history, operations, sales, problems such as bankruptcy filings, and key executuves. These reports can be ordered online at $20 per company.

You can obtain companies' annual reports and financial details through the giant database Lexis Nexis Express for a $25 search fee plus $20 for each report. If you want a more thorough briefing to really sharpen your competive edge, you can request copies of all news articles on a particular company which appeared during the past year for a $25 search fee plus $5 for each article printed. To keep the cost down, you can ask that the search be limited to 5 or 10 articles. You can save even more money if you pay for the search, which uncovers the story headlines and dates, then read the stories free at a library or on the Internet. Material from Lexis Nexis can be sent to you by e-mail, fax, or Federal Express (the last for $15 extra).

For comprehensive analysts' reports and earning estimates for public companies, Standard & Poor's Fax-on-Demand can fax you a research report (about 5 pages) for $3-$9 within minutes after the order is placed.

EMPLOYMENT AGENCIES

Private employment agencies can be either general employment agencies dealing with secretarial, entry-level, non-management and lower-level management positions in numerous industries or specialist agencies dealing with entry-level up to management positions in a specific industry. Agencies that specialize in your industry are recommended if you are beyond entry-level positions, since they will have more jobs appropriate to your experience.

Most private employment agencies require the employer to pay a fee if you are hired. However, be sure to clarify this at the outset. Read carefully any contract you are given. Check if the agency is a member of the National Association of Personnel Consultants, the industry's professional organization. A plus is if the employment counselor is a Certified Personnel Consultant, which signifies that he or she has at least several years of experience as well as professional training.

Beware of agencies that pressure you into signing a contract right away, insist upon an up-front fee, promise a job, or brag about incredibly high placement rates. Anything that sounds too good to be true usually isn't true.

Temporary help agencies, once the bastion of low-paying secretarial and lower-level positions, now supply everything from lawyers and marketing managers to chief financial officers. (See Chapter 10 for more on temp agencies for 40+ job-seekers.) Working as a temp provides a steady paycheck, the chance to brush up on or learn new skills and to make networking contacts. Temping also gives you a feeling of productivity during a period of unemployment and may even serve as a back door approach to finding a job. It's a good idea to request assignments in your field, even if they are lower-level.

State employment agencies will send your résumé to employers who have listed jobs with them in numerous fields. Increasingly, more employers are listing higher-level positions with public agencies than previously. Check with your local office to see what they offer.

EXECUTIVE RECRUITERS

Also known as *headhunters*, executive recruiting firms are hired by companies to find appropriate employees. Many specialize in certain industries and salary levels. In many cases, since a recruiter's job is to know an industry and its players, a recruiter will contact you. You can contact recruiters on your own as well, by sending a cover letter and résumé. Consult directories, such as the *Directory of Executive Recruiters*, found in many libraries, or the membership directory of the Association of Executive Search Consultants, for listings of recruiters and their specialties.

There are two types of executive recruiters: retainer search and contingency search. Retainer search firms are paid a fee for an exclusive assignment to find a candidate for a company, regardless of whether they actually find a candidate who is hired by the company. They specialize in mid- and upper-level management positions. Because they try to find a person who matches a firm's specific needs, chances are retainer firms will set up fewer interviews for you and inform you of fewer job openings. If your present employer uses a retainer firm, this firm will not consider you for jobs. In addition, you will be recommended for only one position at a time. However, interviews you land will be more targeted, since a retainer firm's client has no desire to waste its time and money and see people it does not regard as serious candidates.

Contingency search firms are paid a fee only if a candidate is hired by a client company, and thus are more motivated to "make a match," even if it is not a good fit. Contingency firms also deal with lower-level and middle-level management jobs, technical jobs, and with lower salary levels than retainer firms. The upside of using a search firm: Your résumé will be sent far and wide to companies with relevant job openings. The downside: You may be screening out potential jobs in the process. Employers whom you could have contacted directly will now be required to pay a fee for you. It is unethical, by the way, to pursue an employer once a search firm has alerted you to an opening.

Remember, executive recruiters do not represent you, and thus are not looking out for your best interests. They represent their client companies. The best way to lure the attention of a recruiter is to be employed and have a fairly high profile—from being active in a professional or trade association, writing articles or books, giving lectures, being an interview source for articles, or being helpful to recruiters who have called you to refer potential candidates.

ALUMNI ASSOCIATIONS AND COLLEGE JOB PLACEMENT CENTERS

The "old boy" and "old girl" network is alive and well at college alumni associations, since so many people prefer to hire and work with fellow graduates of their alma mater. Read your alumni magazine, which often runs announcements on job promotions and new positions for alumni. Browse through your alumni directory, which lists names, addresses, and business affiliations of members. Alumni associations sponsor parties, lectures, sports events, vacations, and other social events that offer good networking opportunities. Many colleges have chapters in many different cities, which may be especially helpful if you relocate. Some have university clubs where members can gather for meals, drinks, and events. In addition, some larger colleges also have job placement networks.

If you're in college or a recent graduate, your college job placement center can provide job listings, counselors who can assess your interests and skills, and help in obtaining interviews with on-campus recruiters. Information on internships and career-related materials, résumé writing classes, videotaped mock interviews, and vocational testing on tests like the Meyers-Briggs or the Strong-Campbell Interest Inventory are also offered. It's best to visit the center early and often before May of your senior year and leave a good impression. Many colleges have alumni mentor programs, and keep files of alumni who are willing to advise students about a particular occupation. Most permit alumni of any age to use at least some of their services, including appointments with job counselors, libraries and job listings.

Electronic job hunt resources include:

Career Connections
(415) 903-5800

CompuServe
(800) 848-8199

Career Database
(508) 487-2238

E-Span
(800) 682-2901

Federal Job Opportunity Board
(912) 757-3030

Fedworld
(703) 487-4608

Help Wanted-USA
(through America Online: (800) 827-6364 or through Internet)

Nexis Express
(800) 227-8379

Prodigy
(800) 776-3449

ProNet
(800) 726-0280

Standard & Poor's Fax-on-Demand
(800) 642-2858

CHAPTER TWO

How to Prepare a Résumé

RÉSUMÉS AS SALES TOOLS

If you think of a résumé as an advertisement for yourself, you'll have a better idea of how to plan, write, and organize it.

Like an ad for a new car or perfume, the purpose of a résumé is to sell a product. Your résumé should highlight your strong points, camouflage your weaknesses, catch the eye, and create a winning impression.

The two goals of a résumé are to:

- package your work history and accomplishments in an effective, organized fashion to prepare you for your job hunt and for interviews
- be a sales tool for obtaining interviews

Spend a great deal of time and thought preparing your résumé. Every word should be carefully chosen and crafted. Unlike a job interview—where it takes about four minutes to form a first impression—a résumé may be judged in a 10-second glance, so make your résumé as strong as possible. Think about it, write it, rewrite it, and reshape it over a period of several days until you produce a document which markets you the way you want to be perceived. If you have spent years building a career, you are seriously shortchanging yourself if you expect to distill all your professional experience within a couple of hours. Ideally, show your résumé to friends in similar jobs in the industry you are targeting or to a career counselor for feedback.

Unlike a job application, a résumé is not a place to merely catalog your work experience and education. Take control and make executive decisions on what to leave out, what to put in, and what to emphasize.

15

"Each person is like a snowflake—try to make your uniqueness stand out and shine through," says résumé expert Ruth K. Robbins of Résumés Plus. "But not so trumped up it's almost a turn-off and you're trying to fool them."

Résumés can either be targeted—directed to a specific employer—or untargeted. You may want to have several résumés on hand that highlight different aspects of your background for different employers. Whatever the case, the more you keep your audience in mind when you write your résumé, the more successful you will be in winning interviews and getting jobs.

HOW AND WHEN TO USE DIFFERENT RÉSUMÉ TYPES

CHRONOLOGICAL

The traditional, chronological résumé lists your work experience in reverse chronological order, with your most recent (or current) job first. Dates of employment, responsibilities, and accomplishments go with each company and job title.

Strengths

- employers like its clarity and easy readability
- demonstrates continuous periods of employment
- demonstrates steady career progress
- emphasizes prominent employers
- emphasizes prominent job titles
- looks straightforward and aboveboard, as if you have nothing to hide

Weaknesses

- gaps in employment and frequent job changes are glaringly obvious
- most significant or impressive jobs may not be most recent
- link between jobs held and career objective may not be apparent
- demonstrates stalled career progress or stagnation in one job
- emphasizes unimpressive employers and job titles
- little work experience is also obvious

Best For

Most people, but especially those with continuous work histories and upward progress in their careers who are seeking jobs in the same or similar industries.

Worst For

Job-hoppers, career changers, people with gaps in their employment, and those who have not made steady career progress.

FUNCTIONAL

A functional résumé consolidates skills and responsibilities, describing them in a general way under headings that represent different areas of expertise, instead of job titles. Company names and titles can be left in or out, and employment dates are omitted. The point is to demonstrate the variety of skills groupings without tying them to specific times or companies.

For example, "administration," "teaching," "labor relations," and "budget" may be different skills headings for a school administrator who has taught, negotiated contracts for school systems, and managed budgets. A graphic designer might use headings like "desktop publishing," "computer graphics," and "mechanical artist." For a new business manager in an advertising agency, "new business development," "account management," "administration," and "creative experience" may be appropriate if he or she is a former account supervisor who began as a copywriter.

Note: Many interviewers and recruiters look at functional résumés with an attitude ranging from suspicion that the candidate is hiding something to active dislike. Use them only if absolutely necessary. For example, Richard Linde, vice president at Battalia Winston International, an executive recruiter, says: "Every time I get them, I throw them out. Even if all the information is there, it isn't worth it. Even if you have a checkered career, it's best not to use a functional résumé."

Strengths

- highlights specific abilities instead of jobs
- downplays unimpressive employers or job titles
- glosses over gaps in employment and job-hopping
- demonstrates skills gained from volunteer work, hobbies, and school activities

- demonstrates skills which may not be recent
- can be easily tailored to fit your job objective in ways a chronological résumé cannot
- downplays a zigzag career path or unrelated jobs

Weaknesses

- employers dislike it since it is often confusing and hard to read
- stigma often attached, since its very ease in disguising employment gaps and low-level jobs invites suspicion
- unclear which abilities apply to which jobs
- does not demonstrate career progress
- does not demonstrate which jobs and abilities are recent
- does not highlight impressive employers or job titles

Best For

Job-hoppers, people with employment gaps or stalled career paths, those who have been out of the work force a long time, and career changers.

Worst For

People with a continuous employment record who demonstrate a steady career progress.

COMBINATION

This résumé starts as a functional résumé, grouping skills and responsibilities under broad headings of different areas of expertise, then ends with a brief listing of companies, job titles, and employment dates.

Strengths

- highlights specific abilities instead of jobs
- can be easily tailored to fit your job objective
- downplays unimpressive employers or job titles
- demonstrates skills which may not be recent
- downplays a zigzag career path or unrelated jobs
- includes job chronology so employer can match work history with skill descriptions

Weaknesses

- does not highlight impressive employers or job titles
- can be confusing and hard to read
- downplays career progress
- downplays continuous work history
- may be less effective than a chronological résumé and may raise suspicion where none is justified

Best For

Career changers and recent college graduates.

Worst For

Job-seekers with continuous work histories and career progress and those with impressive employers and job titles, since these are de-emphasized although listed.

CONTENTS: THE BODY OF THE RÉSUMÉ

All résumés, no matter which style you choose, should contain the following crucial information:

1. Personal Information
2. Summary or Job Objective
3. Work Experience
4. Education
5. Work-related Activities

1. PERSONAL INFORMATION

Your name, address, and telephone number should be either at the top, centered, or in the upper right-hand corner. Consider capitalizing your name or using boldface type for your name (or name, address, and telephone number) for emphasis. Other personal data—such as marital status, health, height, weight—should not appear on your résumé.

2. SUMMARY OR JOB OBJECTIVE

A summary or profile offers a brief overview of your major qualifications and key personality traits in a sentence or several sentences, and is recommended since it "positions" you by tightly focusing your résumé. The information—no more than six lines—should be centered under your name, address and telephone number. The sentences, which are written in third person, need not be complete. The first sentence should be the most forceful to give the interviewer a reason to hire you.

> **Example:** Turnaround specialist with 12 years of experience in commercial real estate and banking. Skilled at detecting the problems in marketing, finance, and operations and solving them through strategic analysis and extensive cost-cutting.

A job objective is a brief statement of your goal, which may be used with or in place of the summary. On the downside, listing a specific job objective can actually screen you out of interviews. On the upside, if you are sure about your job goal and many jobs are around with this title, a job objective can be a good idea. Make it snappy and be sure to say what you offer the employer, instead of what you hope the employer offers you.

> **Example:** Account executive position in public relations for a medical/health specialist utilizing my proven track record in TV, radio and print publicity, and newsletter and speech writing in the field of hospital administration.

3. WORK EXPERIENCE

This should be more than a chronicle of jobs you have held and their responsibilities: It should flesh out your summary statement or support your job objective with pertinent details. Follow the motto of salespeople everywhere: Make it easy for your customer to buy. This means describing your background and skills in a way that is interesting, readable, and sets you apart from the crowd, making the weary interviewer sit up, take notice, and scan your résumé for a full 10 seconds.

The way to achieve this is to think carefully about all the activities you performed in your jobs, then analyze their *significance* to your employers. Take a piece of paper and write down what you think you did in your jobs. (Surprise: You have usually done a great deal more than you think.) Recall the things you are proudest of. Remember the reasons you were praised by supervisors or clients and why you received promotions, raises, or awards. Figure out the skills *behind* your activities.

Look at your description with cool objectivity and the mind-set of a harried interviewer who has hundreds of résumés to wade through. Did you demonstrate how you contributed to the goals dear to a company's heart—making money, saving money, saving time, and running more efficiently? Did you differentiate yourself from others holding the same position? If not, write and rewrite your résumé until you translate your activities into accomplishments that are *measurable* and show *value* to an employer. Use numbers and percentages whenever possible; these instantly stand out and send the message that the company was improved during your tenure.

> **Example:** If as a marketing manager you directed a $15 million campaign that included product packaging redesign and a radical shift in advertising strategies that resulted in a threefold increase in market share last year, say so. If you supervised 75 salespeople in the Midwest region, implemented an incentive system so employee turnover dropped 8% in a year, and reported directly to the company president, don't be shy. Perhaps in your administrative support role, you assisted your boss in researching a new market, then wrote detailed memos that became the nucleus of a report presented to management.

A list of accomplishments, with bullets or asterisks next to each one, makes your work experience clear and readable. Use generous spacing and make judicious use of underlining, boldface type, capital letters, and subheads, which draw attention and reduce visual clutter. One powerful format is a paragraph of description under your job titles and employers, with a list of accomplishments underneath. Or just include your list under your titles and employers. Emphasize your most important accomplishments by listing them first and using them to start paragraphs.

Job titles generally go first, followed by employer names on the same line or underneath in chronological résumés. However, if you want to emphasize your job titles instead of your employers, use capitals, boldface, or underlining for effect. If you received promotions in a job, include them in subheads under the employer so they do not look like different jobs. Years employed (not months—unless these are summer jobs or internships) should go on the extreme right; placing them on the extreme left makes them the most prominent feature of the résumé.

In functional résumés, the skill that is most applicable to the position you are seeking should be placed first and emphasized the most.

Eliminate industry jargon (particularly if you are changing careers), describe what business a company is in if it is not well known (this can be done in parentheses), and replace your job title with a more easily understandable, less technical title.

Describe your most recent job in the most detail. Short, punchy, information-packed sentences are best—no more than one major point per sentence. Eliminate the pronoun "I" when starting sentences; begin with a verb or work responsibility.

Opposite is a list of business skills and related work activities to help you assess your own strengths. Use it as a base and see what else you can add. Also included are action verbs, adjectives, and adverbs to help build your résumé.

SKILL LIST FOR SELF-ASSESSMENT

Financial/Organizational

manage budgets/money
prepare financial statements
keep deadlines
organize/classify/process records
coordinate projects

Observational/Analytical

appraise
reason and abstract
assess

Management

manage personnel
delegate responsibility
plan and forecast
design and develop programs
direct and supervise
hire and build teams
implement policies
establish procedures and/or organizational
    structures

Instructional/Educational

teach
train
brief and explain

Helping/Human Relations

counsel and guide
care for others
participate in teamwork
advocate for others

Leadership

lead people
motivate/inspire people
chair meetings
confront problem situations
mediate
sell
negotiate and bargain
initiate
plan and promote change

Communications

write reports/press releases/ads/speeches/letters
speak to groups
edit books/articles/reports
make radio/TV presentations
translate
perform in public
publicize

Working with Things

build
assemble
shape
operate equipment
install
shape

Problem-Solving

gather information
troubleshoot
critique
review
analyze/dissect
organize/classify information
evaluate

ACTION VERBS

managed	supervised
initiated	directed
improved	expedited
expanded	administered
created	completed
developed	conceived
launched	strengthened
produced	established
streamlined	launched
reorganized	originated
implemented	produced
planned	spearheaded
led	guided
generated	increased
reduced	slashed
demonstrated	maximized
recharged	invented
revitalized	redirected
upgraded	achieved
accomplished	consolidated
coordinated	evaluated
modernized	negotiated
pioneered	promoted
solved	targeted
updated	stabilized

ACTION ADJECTIVES AND ADVERBS

proven	substantial
major	significant
efficiently	cost-effective
successfully	rapidly
prominent	comprehensively
innovative	dynamic

4. EDUCATION

List your college, graduate or professional school, community college or certificate program after work experience, together with years attended, degrees, major, honors, and scholarships. The exception is for recent graduates or current students. In that case, list education first on your résumé, and include honors, extracurricular activities, and grade point average (only if it is good). Do not mention your high school diploma.

5. WORK-RELATED ACTIVITIES

Any trade or professional associations you belong to should be included here, as well as any committees you have chaired and seminars or conferences you have organized, since these demonstrate your involvement and commitment to your industry. Professional awards or honors should also be included. Community activities and volunteer work should be mentioned as well, and described in more detail if they are related to your job objective. Listing hobbies is unnecessary unless you are trying to pad a résumé with a minimal work history.

RÉSUMÉ APPEARANCE

Don't spoil a superb work history with an unprofessional-looking résumé. Strive to have both style and substance. Choose white, off-white, or cream 8-½" × 11" bond paper. Your résumé should be typed in black print on a computer with a high-quality printer; while a laser printer is best, a 24-pin letter-quality dot-matrix printer is acceptable. Select a typeface that is clear and easy to read. If you do not have a computer use a copy shop or résumé service to prepare your résumé.

One or two pages is the best length for a résumé. The best rule of thumb is that, like a good short story or poem, it is as long as it should be to convey its message and retain interest. Don't use two pages if you don't need to. Be terse and pithy.

Proofread your résumé *very* carefully. Have another person critique it if possible. A résumé that states you have "excellent speling and grammer," or is accompanied by a cover letter which begins "Dead Mr. Smith" will go nowhere. Nor will a résumé that lists your telephone number with one wrong digit. Make sure your left margin is even, that the résumé does not look too crowded, and that short blocks of type break up the space.

RÉSUMÉ ADVICE FOR JOB-SEEKERS

1. JOB-HOPPERS

- Drop some jobs of very short duration, such as one or two months.
- Use the combination or functional résumé style so the number of jobs and their duration is less glaringly obvious.
- Try to show a career direction with upward progress.

2. CAREER CHANGERS

- Show transferable skills from other jobs—be as creative as possible in comparing your past jobs and current career objective. For example, both may require verbal communication skills, computer literacy, management experience, writing ability, etc.
- List classes or certificate programs in the field you are targeting.
- Show transferable skills or experience from volunteer work or hobbies.
- List professional associations you belong to and articles you have written that may be relevant.

3. BEING "TOO OLD"

- Delete dates, such as college graduation, job duration, military service.
- Minimize dates by placing them after company name and position or in parentheses after position held.
- Don't go back more than 20 years—omit earlier jobs.
- Use a combination or functional résumé style.

4. BEING "OVERQUALIFIED"

- Replace higher-level titles with titles that sound less imposing.
- Omit any advanced degrees.
- Downplay the importance of jobs held.

5. Unemployed or Fired

- Do freelance, consulting, part-time, or volunteer work.
- Omit reasons why you are unemployed (e.g., downsizing, corporate cutbacks, etc.).
- Use a combination or functional résumé style.
- Use a chronological style if your work history is solid, except for your current unemployment.

SAMPLE RÉSUMÉS

The following pages provide résumés that illustrate the themes just discussed.

The first two résumés (before and after) show how a dry job description can be transformed into a dynamic personal statement.

This "before" résumé reads like a dry job description.

ELIZABETH GHAFFARI

207 Dobbs Ferry   Home: (602) 555-1223
Phoenix, AZ 85019

EXPERIENCE

ORANGE COMPUTER SYSTEMS   1988-Present
<u>Director Corporate Communications</u>

Plan and supervise all corporate communications staff and activities for diversified financial information services company on a global basis.

- Develop, direct and implement global media, public relations, and internal-communications programs in support of corporate and sales objectives, working closely with executive management team.

- Direct all media-relations activities related to new product introductions and product enhancements; initiate media contacts; respond to press inquiries; coordinate and conduct interviews; and develop all press materials.

- Develop and direct advertising and promotional literature activities, overseeing all corporate publications, including corporate and product brochures, sales materials, and customer and employee newsletters.

ELECTRONIC DATA SYSTEMS   1986-1988
<u>Manager</u>, Advertising and Promotion

Developed and implemented marketing and promotion strategies for Reuters and its North American subsidiaries.

- Worked with market and product managers to identify opportunities for product and sales promotions and new product development for multiple market
  segments. Conducted market research, developed marketing strategies and implemented tactical plans (e.g. direct response marketing and sales incentive programs).

- Responsible for planning biannual securities analyst meetings and communication product information to investors and industry analysts.

- Orchestrated six product introductions during three-month period, including public-relations activities, promotional literature and training materials.

- Responsible for forecasting and maintaining $4.0 million budget.

- Managed corporate and product advertising programs, hiring and working with various agencies.

ELIZABETH GHAFFARI   Page 2

CREDIT LYONNAIS   1984-1986
<u>**Corporate Investment Officer and Product Manager28**</u>

Planned and directed the sales and promotion efforts for the bank's corporate and correspondent sales staff for a variety of products including foreign exchange and precious metals.

- Developed active and profitable business relationships with correspondent banks for sale of precious metals and foreign exchange products.

- Established and developed new account relationships. Brought in eleven new corporate accounts which produced significant business in precious metals and foreign exchange trading areas.

- Managed market study to identify size, segments and opportunities of various markets. Prepared analysis and recommendations for new product development and trading vehicles.

WASSERELLA & BECKTON   1979-1984
<u>**Director of Marketing**</u>

Managed all activities of the Marketing Department, including product development, sales promotion, advertising and public relations activities for diversified financial services company.

- Conceptualized and developed national marketing strategy for foreign exchange services offered to travel industry professionals via automated airline reservation system.

- Developed and implemented business plans for a variety of products, including responsibility for product positioning, pricing, contracts, advertising and promotional materials.

- Promoted from Foreign Exchange Trader to Marketing Representative to Director of Marketing in three years.

EDUCATION

B.A., Psychology, University of Phoenix   1979

This "after" résumé focuses on Elizabeth Ghaffari's dynamic accomplishments, diversity of experience, and numerous skills.

ELIZABETH GHAFFARI

207 Dobbs Ferry
Phoenix, AZ 85019

Residence: (602)555-1223
Work: (602)555-7889

CORPORATE COMMUNICATIONS EXECUTIVE
with 14 years' experience in

• High-Tech   • Information Services   • Financial Services

Experience includes:

- Global Media and Investor Relations
- Customer Videos and Newsletters
- Advertising/Promotional Literature
- Employee Newsletters
- Employee Roundtables/Awards Programs
- Speech-Writing/Papers/Public Speaking

- **A corporate strategist and key member of the management team** with extensive knowledge of financial markets.

- **A crisis manager**: bringing common sense, organizational skills, and a logical decision-making process to solving sensitive, time-critical problems.

- **A spokesperson for the corporation**: developing and communicating key corporate messages accurately and convincingly, under deadline pressure, to multiple audiences including employees, the media, customers and investors.

Proven team leader and problem solver with highly developed
analytical, organizational, communications, and strategic planning skills.

ORANGE COMPUTER SYSTEMS
Director, Corporate Communications

1988-Present

- Gained extensive positive media coverage in conjunction with launch of company's first product for new market segment.
  - Planned and conducted **media events in 8 countries**.
  - Resulted in **positive stories in 30 major publications** and trade press: *The Wall Street Journal, The New York Times, Barron's, The Financial Times, Forbes,* and various foreign publications.
  - A first for the company, **positive TV coverage in the United States**: CNN, CNBC, **and Europe**: Sky Financial Television, Business Daily, The City Programme.
- Successfully **avoided communications crisis**, gained positive press coverage and customer support when company sold a major division. Within a 60-day period:
  - Planned and managed all aspects of a **13-city, interactive teleconference**.
  - Developed all written materials including various employee and customer communications, background materials and press releases.
  - Wrote speeches for six executives including both company presidents (present and acquiring companies).
  - Wrote and produced an extensive question-and answer document covering **union, compensation and benefits issues and business rational**.
  - Selected and trained staff representatives for each 13 cities.
- Developed and implemented **company's first employee awards program** for service excellence.
  - Honored employees who participated in planning sessions.
  - **Led to changes in key areas** including improvements in software manufacturing efficiencies, shortening of the product development cycle, and improved employee morale.

ELIZABETH GHAFFARI - Page 2

- **Introduced desk-top publishing** program for in-house production of all promotional materials and various customer and employee newsletters.
  - **Reduced outside service expense by 75%.**
  - Created new **corporate standards manual** and reorganized promotional literature system to replace inconsistent product literature.
- Conducted group and individual **employee meetings** to gain and disseminate critical information in identifying and resolving employee-relations problems.
- Prepared quarterly management reports and written/oral presentations to top management and employees to describe corporate accomplishments compared to goals.
- Managed all customer/media/employee communications for sale of three business units.

ELECTRONIC DATA SYSTEMS   1986–1988
__Manager, Advertising and Promotion__

- Prepared written and oral **presentations to boards of directors** and senior managers on various services, concepts and results.
- Planned **product launch** and company participation in global foreign exchange conference. Successful product launch resulted in **generating 450 letters of intent from 1500 participants**. Assured successful product introduction:
  - Developed 5-week **direct-mail campaign** to stimulate interest and create an aura of excitement around product prior to conference. Campaign continued at conference with daily newsletter and door stuffer.
  - Maximized impact of **product demonstrations** through use of compelling visual presentation and environment.
  - **Trained teams** of product demonstrators to assure that information regarding benefits and features would be delivered in consistent way.
- Strengthened company relationships with **industry analysts and investors** by arranging product demonstrations in conjunction with bi-annual industry analyst meetings. Demonstrations stimulated interest and **gained support for strategic direction from investor community** by communicating important strategic and product information.
  - Selected products to be demonstrated, developed promotional materials, organized display area, selected and trained product demonstrators to assure delivery of consistent corporate message.

CREDIT LYONNAIS   1984-1986
__Product Manager__

- Established and developed new account relationships.
  - Brought in **11 new corporate accounts during 10-month period** producing significant business in precious metals and foreign exchange trading areas.

WASSERELLA & BECKTON
__Director of Marketing__

- **Developed breakthrough idea to sell** foreign exchange services (currency and travelers' checks) through travel agents the same way hotel space and airline tickets are sold
  – via automated airline reservation systems.
  - Sold concept to senior management and **negotiated contracts with three major airlines.**
  - Developed sales and operational procedures. **Hired and trained 10-person sales and operations staff.**
  - **Promoted concept to travel agents** across the country through industry trade shows and sales program.

EDUCATION
B.A., Psychology, University of Phoenix, 1979

Barbara Wilson's stint as a consultant nicely fills a two-year gap in corporate experience and is anchored by some prestigious clients.

BARBARA D. WILSON

26 Remsen Street   215-555-5662 (H)
Philadelphia, PA 17678   215-555-6391 (O)

SUMMARY OF QUALIFICATIONS

Seasoned Facilities Management Professional with 15 years of experience both as an Internal and External Consultant for major corporations and nonprofit organizations. Experienced in Space Allocation, Planning/Design, Budget Allocation, and Vendor/Contractor Selection.

- Team Leader with excellent interpersonal and communication skills.
- Creative problem solver with ability to "sell" concepts and solutions.
- Published in major business magazines.

PROFESSIONAL EXPERIENCE

Account Executive   1992–present
ABC Office Center   Philadelphia, PA

- As Project Manager for corporate accounts, sell space planning solutions for complex areas, utilizing appropriate furniture selection.
- Interview clients; determine work and budget requirements; present options and strategies for optimal space planning.
- Research and recommend specific manufacturers.
- Work for clients in the following industries and settings: Accounting, Law, Advertising, Public Relations, and Computers as well as Hospitals, Nonprofits, and U.N. Missions.

Independent Facilities Management Consultant   1990–1992
                                                    Philadelphia, PA

- Contracted as Project Manager by facilities consultants and design firms to handle complex corporate projects.
- Conducted space analysis/allocation studies, reconfiguration of space, field measurements, renovations and vendor selection.
- Negotiated costs and reviewed bid specifications.
- A selection of clients included:
    - *EFG National Bank*, Washington, D.C.: space allocation/analysis for 1,000+ personnel
    - *HIJ Networks*, Baltimore, MD: relocation project
    - *J.W. Thomson*, New York, NY: reconfigured space allocation boundaries of 15,000 sf, plus multiple site lobby renovations
    - *MNO New York/BMG New York*: Project Manager for furniture inventory utilizing bar-code computerized system (900,000 sf project)

BARBARA D. WILSON   215-555-5662 (H)
Page 2   215-555-6391 (O)

Planning Manager/Space Allocation   1987–1990
PQR & Co.   Trenton, NJ

• Created space management system to successfully track 5.7 million sf space inventory.
• Helped reduce real estate expenditures through restacking process (e.g., organization of HQ and other company buildings).
• Prepared detailed budgets for the Design & Development Department.
• Supervised project personnel.

Senior Project Manager   1985–1987
RST Office Supply Co.   Philadelphia, PA

• Managed large furniture open plan systems installations for Fortune 500 clients including DuPont.
• Reviewed floor plans with architects and planned all open system components for 2,400 work stations at DuPont.
• Coordinated production schedules, tracking factory and construction completion.

Project Manager, Interior Design   1979–1985
The Life Assurance Society   Philadelphia, PA

• Hired to manage interior projects from space planning to move-in.
• Interfaced with top senior executives, architects, and relocation companies.
• Executed purchasing and contracting.
• Worked with "executive" clients in selection of furniture, carpeting, wall coverings, artwork, etc.
• During major downsizing, was retained as part of an "inside" team.

EDUCATION

B.F.A., Interior Design   1978
New Jersey Institute of Technology   Newark, NJ

Additional courses in: Business Management; Real Estate Law; Market/Negotiating Office Leases; Sales (Dale Carnegie); Communication; Textile Design.

LANGUAGES

Fluent in French.

PUBLICATIONS

"Determining Space Needs, etc."   June 1986
The Office Magazine

"When Is a Square, etc.?"   April 1986
Crain's New York Business

NEIL RAYMOND

520 Columbus End Avenue
New York, NY 10024
(212) 888-7777

Senior Commodities Trader
with international experience and contacts in plastics, petrochemicals, industrial raw materials and food products.

- Confident in taking positions (long or short) in rapidly moving markets.

- Specialize in locating "hard-to-find" products worldwide.

- Able to communicate and negotiate effectively in several languages and multiple cultural and economic environments.

SPECIAL SKILLS:

Fluent in French and Spanish. Working knowledge of German, Italian and Arabic.

PROFESSIONAL EXPERIENCE:

MANAGER, SENIOR TRADER (Plastics Specialist)   1990-present
Leverage Industries Group, Inc., New York, NY
A Chemical and Plastics Trading Company with offices in The Middle East, Far East and Europe

Accomplishments :

- Responsible for increase in Plastics Department sales from less than $100,000 annually to over $3 million with average return of 10%. Expanded product line to include all Polyolefins and some engineering resins.

- Successfully closed trades and grew market base in South America, Far East, Middle East and French-speaking African territories.

- Managed and monitored plastics purchasing and sales in company's overseas offices.

- In addition to Plastics, also created markets for Industrial Chemicals, including polyurethane chemicals, cement additives, leather tanning chemicals, paint/pigments intermediates. Achieved average returns of 20-30%.

- Established contracts with major American (North and South), European and Far East Petrochemical Companies for exclusive representation of their respective products in Greece and Singapore.

- Supervised and coordinated all aspects of each transaction including international documentation, transportation and negotiation, and execution of all purchases and sales contracts.

- Skilled at executing trades and taking positions in major foreign currencies.

- Established outstanding working relationships with international sales managers and key market players worldwide. Called on overseas customers and suppliers throughout Europe and North Africa.

- Represented company at International Plastics and Chemical trade shows in Germany, France and the U.S. several times annually. Initiated and developed new business resulting from leads from these events.

NEIL RAYMOND
-2-

IMPORT AND DOMESTIC SALES EXECUTIVE   1988-1990
BARRY UHE Company, Secaucus, NJ
Importer and distributor of pharmaceutical raw materials and fine chemicals.

Accomplishments:

- Purchased pharmaceutical raw materials overseas for import and distribution in U.S. market.
- Procured food processing chemical overseas and domestically and sold to pet food and food additive companies in U.S. market.
- Assisted in buying of commodity chemicals from U.S. producers for export.

ASSISTANT TRADER/ INDUSTRIAL CHEMICALS   1987-1988
AEF Group, New York, NY
Chemical Trading Firm with offices in the Far East, Europe and Russia

Accomplishments:

- Sourced, bought and sold commodity chemicals in tight markets.
- Averaged 15% profit on sales of industrial chemicals worldwide.
- Established new product lines and expanded markets in the Far East.

EXPORT ANALYST   1986-1987
STS Services, New York, NY
World's largest international export inspection organization

ASSISTANT MARKETING COORDINATOR/TRAFFIC MANAGER   1983-1985
Food Products Division, Gulf & Western Americas Corporation, New York, NY

ASSISTANT TRAFFIC MANAGER   1978-1982
Nowell Brothers, Inc. (currently Filco, Inc.), New York, NY

ASSISTANT TRAFFIC MANAGER/TRADER'S ASSISTANT   1976-1978
Associated Metals & Minerals Corporation, New York, NY

EDUCATION:

Bucknell University, PA
B.A. Degree in Romance Languages

University of Paris, France

John Lander's résumé shows a career-changer who is seeking to move from a dental clinician—both as a self-employed dentist and managing partner of a dental center—to an executive position in managed care.

John H. Lander, D.D.S.
10 Fair Lawn Drive
Seattle, Washington 95403
206-555-8202

Objective: **Successful Clinician** with strong career interests and experience in Health Care Management seeking position analyzing and evaluating Health Care Plans offered by large and mid-sized firms to their employees.

Profile:
- Eight years as Managing Partner of large multi-chair clinic
- Demonstrated ability to evaluate and orchestrate effective solutions to complex problems
- Exceptional communication and management skills
- Well versed in all aspects of office operations, from community outreach to billing, accounting, and supervising staff
- Familiarity with the details of Health Care Administration and Insurance plans

Licensure: Washington State license in Dentistry

Professional Experience:

1985–present **Managing Partner**, STX DENTAL CENTER, Seattle, WA
Established a dental office servicing the Seattle indigent population. Developed marketing strategies to maintain patient flow.

- Administered third-party payment and collection systems
- Developed and implemented a software program to incorporate billing, scheduling, and analysis of specialized accounting information
- Supervised staff of fourteen, including dentists, hygienists, and six office assistants
- Examined patients and presented treatment plans
- Evaluated the financial and tax needs of the practice and monitored accounting procedures

1981–1984 **Solo Practitioner**, Portland, OR
- Maintained a high-quality, fee-for-service practice, specializing in complete oral rehabilitation.

John H. Lander, D.D.S.   **Page 2**

**Related
Experience:**

1976–1978   **Chairman of the Science Department**
THE AMERICAN SCHOOL OF VENICE, Venice, Italy
Supervised and developed science curriculum for American High
School students studying in Italy. Maintained position concurrent with
medical studies.

1975–1976   **Partner-Consultant**
INTERMED, Seattle, WA
Worked in nonprofit organization which facilitated placement of
American Pre-Med students into European Medical Schools.

1969–1971   **Customer Service Representative/Troubleshooter**
GHI SECURITIES, Seattle, WA
At early age, was given increasing responsibilities for researching and
reconciling problematic financial accounts. Dealt extensively with the
public and upper management.

Education:

1978–1981   WASHINGTON STATE COLLEGE OF DENTISTRY, D.D.S.
Seattle, Washington

1975–1978   UNIVERSITY OF PADUA MEDICAL SCHOOL
Padua, Italy

1975   BELLINGHAM COLLEGE
Bellingham, Washington
B.S., Biochemistry

Languages: Fluent in Italian and Spanish. Working knowledge of French.
Extensive travel throughout Europe and North Africa.

Architect Carl Mundy's résumé lists major details of specific projects first, then follows with accomplishments, roles, and tasks.

CARL MUNDY, R.A.
319 Lake Shore Drive
Chicago, IL 60611
(312) 555-9576

ARCHITECT• MANAGER

PROFILE:

Sixteen years of experience in design and construction with portfolio of successful, nationally recognized projects. Skilled in strategic planning, project management, and financial analysis.

Demonstrated strengths:
• Implementation and Direction of Complex Systems and Schedules
• Intensive Negotiation with Tenant/Landlord/Contractors
• Management of Professional Staff

PROFESSIONAL EXPERIENCE:

XYZ Construction Corporation   1986-present
PROJECT EXECUTIVE (1993-present) – The Construction Management Joint Venture, a consortium agent for the Health and Hospitals Corporation, in the construction of a $200 million turnkey project at QRS Hospital Center.

SENIOR PROJECT MANAGER (1992) – Carol Stream Hospital Center.

PROJECT MANAGER (1991) – $45 million, 25-story hotel and commercial building in downtown Chicago.

PROJECT MANAGER (1989-1990) – $89 million, 46-story steel and reinforced concrete hotel over landmark Detroit theater.

PROJECT MANAGER (1988) – $50 million worth of contracts on a 50-story, superblock, multi-use Chicago project.

ASSISTANT PROJECT MANAGER (1986-1987) – Promoted within a year to full project manager.
• Built high-rise hotel at budget and ahead of schedule. Administered the leasehold improvement agreement from design through occupancy. The interiors of the 25 story building won a "Gold Key Award" in *Hospitality Design Magazine*. Managed the worlds's largest single signage installation which became the subject of a National Geographic Television special.
• Renegotiated an expiring agreement for an additional $20 million of construction management services and a three and a half year extension. Negotiated takeover arrangements for a contractor bankruptcy ($5 million) and reduced schedule delay from six months to three months. Recaptured over $1 million of previously unfunded office expenditures.
• Administered over 50 contracts and restructured project management staff for development of Hospital Center. Completed several turnkey departments to meet schedule and maintain budget.

CARL MUNDY (312)555-9576

- Assumed the management of an interior redesign, midstream during the construction phase of 46-story hotel. Reestablished schedule and budget, bringing interior project to completion at original, anticipated cost. Assembled a complex 150' long truss over an existing landmark which earned a cover story in *Engineering News Record.*
- Assigned to Center City Plaza site midway into steel erection, salvaging a failing contractor from bankruptcy and restructuring the organization to produce the contracted job. Coordinated the installation of the largest copper clad roof in Chicago. The project was featured in *Engineering News Record* cover story, a full-length book, and a five-hour public television series on high rise construction.
- Resolved the business and production problems with a structural steel fabricator to ensure a timely erection completion. Coordinated all mechanical trades and installations. Closed out contractor accounts.
- Directed and managed a staff of thirty including office support personnel.

SJC Design Build, Ltd. 1984-1985
PARTNER AND MANAGING PRINCIPAL in a Development/Construction firm.

Albert Mann, A.I.A. 1982-1983
ARCHITECT AND DESIGNER at a large scale residential/commercial waterfront development.

Frank A. Vole, P.E. 1978-1981
DESIGNER/OFFICE MANAGER AND SUPERINTENDENT for small architectural engineering design-build firm.

EDUCATION AND LICENSING:

Illinois Institute of Technology
BACHELOR OF SCIENCE IN ARCHITECTURE, 1979

ILLINOIS STATE LICENSED ARCHITECT

AFFILIATIONS:

Member, **American Institute of Architects**
Member, **Council of Architects, Engineers & Surveyors of Chicago**
Illinois State Society of Architects

Robert Finch's résumé lists numerous diverse accomplishments as an experienced investor relations professional.

Robert Finch
2181 Starling Way
Alpine, NJ 07642
(201) 555-1423

. . . .

Summary:

Investor Relations professional with over 10 years of experience in domestic and overseas markets. Expertise in NASDAQ and AMEX securities. Proven sales ability with outstanding presentation and communication skills.

Professional Experience:

- Established effective relationships with money managers and brokers. Through face-to-face interactions with key decision makers, created climate of responsiveness and trust.
- Built professional rapport with financial analysts through group presentations, informational meetings, and social gatherings to articulate positive institutional image.
- Established national data base of brokers and money managers.
- Initiated numerous marketing projects such as direct mail campaigns and financial surveys for lead generation, which resulted in overall increased revenues to client firms.
- Expert in private placements, especially those pursuant to Regulation 504-D. Knowledgeable in 144 trading procedures.
- Interfaced with publishers and editors of newspapers, newsletters, and financial press. Organized press conferences and wrote press releases and "infomercials".
- Represented companies at international and national financial conferences and trade shows.
- Acted as liaison with syndication departments in both major and boutique firms.
- Major sales producer: able to call "cold" throughout the world.

Work History:
1990-present

ABC CAPITAL PARTNERS, New York, NY
Investor Relations Executive
Responsible for planning, developing, and marketing concepts for client companies on the AMEX and NASDAQ.

1987-1990   EFC ASSOCIATES, New York, NY
Investor Relations
Located market makers for publicly traded companies. Contacted financial media in order to feature clients in newsletters, cable, network TV, and print.

1986-1987   FIRST COMMERCE SECURITIES, Amsterdam, The Netherlands
Investor Liaison
Introduced the European community of investors, brokers, bankers, and financial media to American and Canadian securities. Traded foreign currencies for firm.

1981-1986   BLINDER, ROBINSON SECURITIES, New York, NY
Licensed Stockbroker (Series 7)
Promoted from stockbroker to East Coast Publicity Director. Initiated new projects which helped company become the leading OTC house in the industry.

Education:
1980-1981   LONG ISLAND UNIVERSITY, Brooklyn, NY
M.B.A. program

1976-1980   FLORIDA INTERNATIONAL UNIVERSITY, Miami, Florida
Bachelor of Science, Management

CHAPTER THREE

How to Look Your Best at an Interview

The four-minute test is critical when you go on a job interview. According to studies, that's the time frame in which a first impression is created when we meet someone. In fact, opinions start to be formed about our intelligence, professionalism, background, and ethics within 10 seconds or less. Within 30 seconds, the interviewer has already assimilated a great deal of information from clothing, eye contact, body language, voice, and choice of words.

A first impression has great staying power, and is a powerful thing to counteract. Because of what social scientists have dubbed the "halo effect," a person will look for evidence to affirm an initial positive impression in the rest of the encounter. A negative impression can be overcome, but it will be difficult.

"You usually don't get a second chance—so if you strike out on your first impression, it's tough to get back on the good side of your interviewer," says Carolyn Mann, an executive development consultant.

An interview—and ultimately, a job offer—is the goal of your job search, and may be the product of weeks of mailing out résumés and cover letters, research, networking, meetings with executive recruiters or employment agencies, and preparation. Therefore, you should do everything in your power to convey an image of competence, polished professionalism and reliability through your dress, body language, and voice in those first four minutes. While substance should win out over style, the fact is that attractive, well-dressed and well-groomed people are more apt to be hired. Thus, it is vitally important to look and act the best you possibly can so your efforts toward substance will not be marred by a careless approach to style.

"Image is the easiest thing to manipulate—the fastest, least expensive, and with the biggest immediate payoff," says Virginia Sullivan, president of Image Communications International, a New York image consulting firm that counsels many Fortune 500 companies.

Enhancing your image is faster, cheaper, and often more effective than going for an MBA or diction lessons, she notes. "It's not just fluff—it's an issue of self-esteem. Your image affects not only how people treat you, but how you feel about and carry yourself."

Color, dress, style, and body language are simply weapons in our arsenal that we can be trained to use to our best advantage. All should send out a single consistent message to the interviewer. Confident words should not be undercut by shifty or defensive body movements, and a highly professional manner should not be compromised by slovenly or overly casual dress or grooming, for example.

Hands and shoes are the two most telling nonverbal cues interviewers notice, says Ms. Sullivan. As the expression goes, "God is in the details," she notes. "As your hands are, your life is. Hands are one of the things we neglect when we feel poorly about ourselves." Bitten fingernails and jagged cuticles reveal how nervous and lacking in confidence we are and belie a cool demeanor. Scuffed shoes with run-down heels betray a lack of attention to detail.

DRESSING FOR THE INTERVIEW

Don't be like the entertainment lawyer who wore a black leather micro-miniskirt to an interview at a law firm. The only thing about her the interviewer remembered was the leather mini. Similarly, a banker with a background in theater arrived at an interview at a foreign bank clad in a Prairie skirt, off-shoulder tunic, and boots. "This is me—why should I appear to be something I'm not?" she told Ms. Mann. Not surprisingly, neither candidate got the job.

The way you look at an interview will never get any better on the job, interviewers assume. Therefore, if you don't take the time and effort to present yourself in the best possible light, employers may conclude you will display similar ill-preparedness on the job.

"The way you dress is the single most important nonverbal communication you make about yourself," says Tom Jackson in his book *Guerrilla Tactics in the Job Market.*

Dress for the job you want—not the one you have—is excellent advice for both interviews and on-the-job situations. "Nothing succeeds like the appearance of success," Christopher Lasch notes in his book *The Culture of Narcissism.* You can't err by dressing a bit on the conservative side—you can always express your flair for style later, when you are comfortably ensconced in the job.

"You have to make the choice, 'I'm comfortable in this look,'" says Ms. Mann. "Remember, the company won't change. You are the one who will have to conform to the company's style. You may be stuck in an environment you would be unhappy in."

One clue is to look through the company's annual report to see how employees dress—or to stand by the elevator and observe employees as they come and go. Don't let the dress-down trend popular at many big companies, including IBM, fool you into dressing casually at the interview, however. While casual dress is now permitted in many companies—on Fridays, perhaps, or even all the time—this is a perk reserved for employees, not applicants.

A lot more latitude in dress exists today for job-seekers, particularly for women. "We don't have to just wear navy blue suits with floppy bow ties the way we were advised in the 1970s anymore," says Ms. Sullivan. "Many women in corporate America are scared to look feminine, and suffer from what I call the 'too' syndrome—they feel they are too fat, too small, too old. However, looking dowdy is never going to work in your favor." A splash of red, or even a red suit—which signifies power, authority, confidence, and sexuality—may be just right for a woman seeking a high-level position in a creative profession, she notes.

Always stand before a full-length mirror wearing your interview attire before an interview. Check meticulously for stains and spots, loose hanging threads, loose buttons, unattractive tightness or slackness, frayed areas, wrinkles, baggy stockings or stockings with runs, and worn-down or unpolished shoes.

Use "optical illusion dressing" to accentuate any assets you have and camouflage your limitations. This does not mean you should flaunt your sexuality. However, a slim waistline can be shown off by wearing a jacket with more waist definition; shapely legs can be showcased with a slightly shorter skirt; a slender neck can be adorned with a long strand of pearls, Ms. Sullivan advises women. Colors should be chosen carefully so they flatter your natural assets.

A signature style piece—such as a vividly colored silk scarf, striking necklace or pin for women, and braces or suspenders, ties, or socks for men—is recommended. This shows you took time to pull yourself together, makes you stand out and not look cookie-cutter, and can even serve as a conversation piece, Ms. Sullivan says.

DRESSING AND GROOMING ADVICE FOR MEN AND WOMEN

MEN

DO'S

DO wear a suit, preferably wool (in warm weather, a tropical-weight wool is fine). Avoid sports jackets or blazers, which are too casual for interview attire, and polyester, which tends to look inexpensive.

DO wear suits in dark blue or gray (charcoal or light). Pinstripes are fine, but avoid brown, black, or brightly colored suits.

DO wear a white, off-white, or pale blue long-sleeved shirt in cotton or a cotton blend, which offers the crispest, most professional look and absorbs perspiration better than synthetics. The shirt should be ironed and starched, despite what the label says. Avoid patterned shirts.

DO wear subdued, quality cufflinks if your shirt has French cuffs.

DO wear a tie in a solid color—such as navy, red, maroon, or yellow—stripe, paisley or foulard-type print. The tie should be silk or a silk-and-wool blend, and should be clean, unwrinkled, and well-knotted. The width should be roughly the width of your lapels. Avoid bowties, too-wide ties, vivid designs, and wool, synthetic, or linen ties.

DO wear leather dress shoes in black or brown. Lace-up wingtips or slip-ons are fine. Make sure shoes with laces are tied securely.

DO make certain your shoes are well polished. Avoid worn-down heels and soles, which create a shabby appearance (hence the phrase "down-at-the-heels").

DO wear as expensive a watch as you can afford.

DO wear dress socks in a color that matches your suit. Knee-highs are best, to avoid a flash of leg between the top of your socks and the bottom of your pants.

DO carry a leather briefcase or attaché case in burgundy or brown, which adds to a professional appearance.

DO wear a belt in the same color as your shoes—or a complementary color.

DO take a handkerchief or tissue with you. You never know when you may sneeze, and it's embarrassing to have to ask for a tissue.

DO wear a coat in beige or blue, if the weather demands it, or a trench coat in beige or light brown.

DO make sure your hair is clean, well trimmed, and well groomed.

DO get a close shave beforehand, but be careful about nicks.

DO make sure your nails are meticulously clean and well trimmed.

DON'TS

DON'T wear casual or novelty watches—such as big sport watches with plastic wristbands, cartoon figure clockfaces, etc.

DON'T wear too much jewelry.

DON'T wear monograms. Some people think they send an elitist message.

DON'T proclaim your religious, political, or fraternity affiliation in your jewelry or other accessories, since they may send the wrong message.

DON'T sport facial hair. Beards are out; mustaches are a gray area. If you have a mustache, make sure it is well trimmed.

DON'T wear a handkerchief in your breast pocket.

DON'T let dandruff on your shoulders or collar ruin an otherwise meticulous appearance.

WOMEN

DO'S

DO wear a tailored suit or a dress with a jacket. A jacket makes a strong statement, and you should not go to an interview without one. While your look should be business-like and not overly feminine, you needn't be a male clone wearing the female "dress for success" suit in vogue some years ago—navy blue suit and a white blouse with a front tie bow. Women can exercise more latitude in this area than men can, and can look stylish but within reasonable limits.

DO choose suits in conservative solid colors such as gray (charcoal, medium, or light), navy blue, black, beige, or camel. Natural fibers, such as wool or linen, are your best bets; most synthetic blends, no matter how attractive, give off a whiff of the bargain basement to the sharp eye of an interviewer. In industries such as fashion, entertainment, advertising, and public relations, you can display a bit more creativity in your dress—but not much.

DO wear hemlines on the conservative side. Hemlines rise and fall in the fashion industry—but not in the job interview world. A hemline at the knee, slightly above or below the knee is best—no very short skirts if you want to be taken seriously.

DO wear leather shoes in black, brown, navy blue, maroon, or beige. Heels of less than two inches or flats are fine—teetering on too-high heels is out of place at a job interview and, besides, you may trip. Conservative pumps are best, but sling-back shoes are also acceptable. Check to make sure heels and soles are not worn down.

DO wear stockings in natural shades—beige, nude, or taupe are best. Avoid dark colors with light-colored shoes or suntan shades, which look unnatural. Always carry a spare pair in your purse or briefcase, since stockings are likely to run at the worst possible times. It is endlessly embarrassing—not to mention distracting to the interviewer—to keep shifting in your seat to avoid displaying a huge run or hole.

DO wear a scarf in silk or a high-quality synthetic in a stylish yet fairly subdued pattern or solid color if you choose to add a scarf as a finishing touch.

DO wear subdued, tasteful jewelry. Pearl, stud, button, or other small earrings are acceptable. A simple pearl or gold necklace, bracelet, and ring are also fine—but make sure your jewelry enhances, and does not overwhelm, your outfit.

DO carry a leather briefcase, if possible. It creates a professional look and makes a "power" statement.

DO carry an attractive handbag, as expensive as you can afford. Bags that are inexpensive-looking or too big and tote-bag-like can be turnoffs.

DO sport a simple, attractive hairstyle. Go light on the hairspray and styling. If your hair is quite long—past shoulder-length—consider pulling it back or putting it up in a bun or French twist.

DO make sure your nails are clean, well-trimmed, fairly short, and, if possible, freshly manicured. Light-colored polish, not dragon lady red, is best. Overly long or jagged nails are turnoffs for professional positions. Use tips to conceal bitten fingernails.

DO wear subtle cosmetics with a well-blended, polished look. No one element—blush, eye makeup, lipstick—should overpower your face. Strike a happy medium between looking noticeably made-up and totally natural.

DO glance at a mirror right before the interview. This is the time to detect smeared eye makeup or lipstick, windswept hair, stocking runs, and other casualties.

DON'TS

DON'T wear anything flamboyant, trendy, or faddish. You are not trying to make a fashion statement, but trying to get a good job.

DON'T wear slacks, even pantsuits.

DON'T have your hair or bangs falling into your eyes or face.

DON'T wear anything low-cut, too tight or short, or otherwise provocative.

DON'T wear sandals, very high heels, unusual colors, or casual styles.

DON'T ever go to an interview bare-legged, even if the temperature is 100 degrees in the shade.

DON'T wear stockings with patterns, lace, bold colors, or seams.

DON'T wear heavy perfume.

DON'T wear an ankle bracelet.

PERSONAL HYGIENE

Make it comfortable for the interviewer to be in the same room with you. Be sure to shower the morning of the interview, apply deodorant, brush your teeth, and use mouthwash. This is particularly important because the anxiety that is natural before an interview can stimulate more perspiration. A squeaky-clean feeling will help to bolster your self-confidence.

BODY LANGUAGE

An astonishingly high percentage of the message we communicate to others is through our nonverbal signals, and not the words we speak. In fact, according to a study of communications by psychologist Albert Mehrabian, 7 percent of a message about our attitudes and feelings derives from our words, 38 percent from our voice, and 55 percent from our facial expressions.

When two people meet for the first time and a positive impression is formed, it is based initially upon a person's physical look. Soon, however, a "dynamic attractiveness" builds, based on the way the person moves and expresses himself or herself, a study by a California State University psychology professor found.

Your body language should convey the same message of professionalism and competence as your words, appearance, and dress. Discordant signals only make the interviewer ill at ease and likely to question the sincerity of your remarks.

Start sending positive signals from the moment you rise to meet the interviewer. Stand straight, with an erect, shoulders-back posture; and greet your interviewer with an open, confident smile and shake hands.

The handshake should be firm enough to inspire trust and confidence. A limp handshake leaves an impression of weakness and vacillation. On the other hand—no pun intended—you don't want to leave the interviewer wincing in pain. The idea is to mirror the pressure used by the interviewer.

Mirroring, in fact, is a good technique to employ throughout the interview, and one used often by salespeople. Take voice, for example. You should try to match the pace of the interviewer's voice. If the interviewer talks very slowly, you should attempt to slow down your own speech, to make him or her feel more comfortable. If the interviewer speaks very fast, try to speed up your conversation, so he or she does not find you a bit "slow." Similarly, if the interviewer speaks in a formal, decorous fashion, mirror this and leave out any slang or colloquial remarks you might otherwise use. If the interviewer laughs, laugh along—at a pitch below him or her.

You get the picture. Mirroring the other person's signals builds rapport. People like to be with—and tend to hire—people similar to themselves, whom they can relate to easily.

Videotaping yourself—and watching your gestures and demeanor as you answer questions you have prepared—will reveal many surprises about how you come across (some negative, I'm afraid). An invaluable tool in learning how to communicate effectively, videotaping is often used by business schools and corporations to fine-tune a person's presentation and performance. "It's a rather remarkable revelation for most people of blatant flaws—facial expressions, figures of speech—which are readily noted by everyone else except themselves, but which are easily correctible," says Richard Linde, vice president of Battalia Winston International, an executive search firm.

Body language along with the messages it sends about honesty and deception is taken very seriously by the police, FBI, and psychologists, as well as interviewers.

Negative Body Signals

- Crossed or folded arms signify defensiveness and a closed attitude.
- Moving your hand to a facial feature—such as your nose or mouth—often means a person is insincere or outright lying, shielding his or her face from spoken untruths.
- Fidgeting—such as twisting or pulling your hair, picking bits of lint from your clothing, persistent foot-swinging (or pen- or foot-tapping), repeatedly clearing your throat, or drumming your fingers on a table signify nervousness, stress, and sometimes boredom.
- Shifting your gaze away from the interviewer while you are talking—or he or she is talking—shows shiftiness or discomfort with what is being discussed.
- Staring persistently is discomfiting and can signify aggressiveness.
- Fiddling with your tie or other article of clothing shows insecurity.
- Crossing a leg so an ankle rests over the other knee shows obstinacy.
- Folding hands behind your head shows arrogance.
- Frowning shows discomfort or annoyance.
- Continual smiling sends a message of weakness, pliability, or insincerity.
- Frozen smiles signify tension.
- Biting your lips signifies stress or insincerity.
- Slouching signifies depression.
- Breathing in short, rapid breaths signifies frustration.
- Doodling on a notepad shows boredom.

Positive Body Signals

- Good eye contact—without staring—only briefly breaking your gaze to look at a notepad, other parts of the interviewer's face, or to the side signifies trustworthiness, alertness, confidence, and reliability.
- Good posture and sitting comfortably on your chair signifies poise and a take-charge attitude.
- Open-handed, palms-up gestures signify sincerity and openness.
- Sitting with uncrossed legs also shows openness.
- "Steepling" one's fingertips signifies confidence.
- Nodding your head slowly now and then—not bobbing your head up and down impatiently—shows thoughtful listening.

CHAPTER FOUR

Types of Interviews and How to Prepare for Them

Many job-seekers believe there is only one type of interview—stressful. Stressful beforehand, due to the jitters of anticipation, and stressful during—much like a dentist appointment, an ordeal to be endured that hopefully will be over soon and will not be repeated until the distant future.

Interviews actually come in different shapes and styles. The purpose of an interview may be different—screening versus selection versus informational. The format may vary—one-on-one versus a group. The location may be an office, a restaurant, or on the telephone. The style may deliberately be a "stress" interview, or not. Your interviewer may be a human resources professional—if the company is large enough to have a personnel department—or a manager or supervisor, or even the owner, if the company is smaller.

Knowing what to expect is crucial so you can adequately prepare, approach the interview in an intelligent fashion, and find no surprises. One thing you can definitely expect: a greater number of interviews within a company than in previous years—from two to eight or even more. The multiple interviews may all be in the course of one grueling day, or staggered over the course of several weeks. Your chances of landing a job after one interview today are exceedingly rare. If you do so, count yourself among the very, very lucky few.

SCREENING INTERVIEWS

The purpose of the screening interview is to weed out—or screen—job-seekers who do not meet basic qualifications of experience and skills for the job. Job-seekers who pass muster are then sent on for further interviews with managers or supervisors in the company who are more closely connected to the job opening. Usually conducted by a human resources professional—often with formal training in interview skills—the screening interview probes for facts and facts alone.

The interviewer will seek to verify facts on your résumé, obtain more facts, and detect exaggerations or outright lies in your responses or your résumé. Because of this "just the facts, ma'am" approach, the interviewer has no interest in your personality traits, attitude, goals or thought processes. Since he or she does not have the power to hire—and will not be working with you—the interviewer does not have to rely on a gut feeling about your desirability as a candidate.

Bearing this in mind, you should politely and directly offer the facts the interviewer seeks, and refrain from volunteering additional information. Save this for the more searching questions which will be asked in later interviews. The screening interviewer is casting about for ways to disqualify and reject you so you never reach this next step. Therefore, allow him or her to take charge of the interview and respond accordingly.

SELECTION INTERVIEWS

Unlike the screening interviewer, the person conducting a selection interview is not an interview professional and usually has no training whatsoever in conducting interviews. Generally, the selection interviewer is a manager or supervisor more familiar with the job and may be your prospective boss. He or she is busy all day long performing his or her own job and is likely to regard the interview as an intrusion into the workday. The interviewer's mind may be preoccupied and a bit frantic not only with the demands of his or her own job, but with the chore of finding a suitable employee—and fast.

Since this interviewer is likely to be working closely with the employee hired and is looking for the right person to fill the job—in contrast to the screening interviewer, who is looking for the wrong people, and ditching them fast—he or she tends to operate from gut instinct. As a result, close attention will be paid to how you think, what you say, how you dress and act, etc. Your best tactic is to exert more control over the content and flow of a selection interview, be more expansive in your responses, and volunteer relevant information since the decision to be made will be a personal one—not one wedded to the bare facts on your résumé. Tips on how to read the interviewer, and respond accordingly, can be found at the end of this chapter.

INFORMATIONAL INTERVIEWS

One of the keys to successful networking, informational interviews involve talking to people in an industry or specific company to gather job leads or other useful information. They are an excellent way to build a resource bank of people who may actually scout for job opportunities for you, and thus uncover the "hidden" job market. Informational interviews can be arranged at any stage of a career—to get started in an industry for neophyte job-hunters, to investigate other industries for job-changers, and to obtain higher-level positions for more senior job-hunters.

You hold the interview and ask most of the questions in an informational interview, turning the tables on the traditional interview. To arrange these interviews, you either call referrals given to you through networking, or cold-call or write letters to specific people in the industry. Indirectness is the best approach. Do not ask directly if a job is available, but ask for specific advice about job opportunities, industry trends, and names of other people to contact.

When you call to arrange an interview, get to the point immediately—introduce yourself, mention the source who referred you (if any), explain the purpose of your call, and ask for a brief meeting at the person's convenience. At the beginning of the interview, repeat the purpose of your meeting and the referral source, in case the person has forgotten. Say something like: "Thank you for taking the time to see me today. I am in the process of exploring several job possibilities. I know what I do well and what I enjoy doing. But before I make any decisions, I am trying to benefit from the advice of individuals such as yourself who have a lot of experience in this area. I am especially interested in learning more about opportunities, necessary skills, responsibilities, advantages, and the future outlook for your field."

Ask clearly defined questions which show you have done your homework, and state your goal and the status of your job search. Tailor your questions as closely as possible both to the person's area of expertise and your skills and background.

Some sample questions to ask are:

- How did you get into this field?
- What do you like most about your job?
- Describe a typical day for you at work.
- What is the standard salary range for an entry-level job in this field?
- What is the best education/training for your job?
- What is the typical career path?
- What industry publications do you recommend?

- What are the major growth areas in your industry?
- What are the major issues/problems facing your industry today?
- What might be the best way to approach prospective employers?
- Is there anyone else you recommend I speak with in your field? May I use your name?

When closing the interview, use dialogue like this: "Thank you so much for your time. I have learned a great deal today. Your advice was very helpful. Is there anyone else you can recommend I speak with who might be willing to meet with me? While I know you may not be aware of any job openings at present for someone with my qualifications, I would appreciate if you could keep me in mind should you hear of any. Thank you again."

Afterward, send a personalized thank you note—you can highlight a noteworthy point made in the interview, or mention what you plan to do with advice given you. Keep in periodic touch by short calls informing the person how his or her advice worked out, asking more specific questions, or sharing information you have gleaned which may be useful to him or her.

Helpful Tips

1. Do not ask for specific advice in your initial phone call. Your goal is a meeting, which potentially may lead to an ongoing relationship.
2. Do be prepared and proactive. Do your homework on the industry, company, and person you are meeting, and frame clear questions as well as a succinct statement about your career goal and job search.
3. Do not enclose a résumé if you send a letter asking for a meeting. Bring it with you to the informational interview—or mail it with a thank you note afterward.
4. Do not ask outright for a job. Ask for information.
5. Do not be discouraged if told there are no job openings. This is not why you're here. Perhaps a job will open up in the future, or a referral from the person you are meeting with will tell you about one. Or you may learn a nugget of information which will greatly aid your job hunt.
6. Do not expect the meeting to last more than a half hour.
7. Do take notes during the meeting on information and referrals offered.
8. Do not get so excited if a job opening is mentioned that you ignore

asking for more general information and referrals. The most likely scenario is that you will end up with no job and no information.

9. Do behave as if this is a formal job interview.
10. Do ask for names and phone numbers of referrals to contact.
11. Do ask if you can use the person's name when you contact these referrals.
12. Do not be discouraged if no referral sources are offered. Most likely, you have learned other valuable information in the interview.
13. Do write a thank you note afterward.
14. Do keep in touch to preserve the relationship. Call with relevant questions or share information learned in your job search. Or send newspaper or magazine clips on the industry which may be of interest with a "FYI" note.
15. Do develop new contacts while preserving old ones.
16. Do be ready to conduct the interview by telephone if the person does not want a meeting.
17. Do ask if you can send your résumé to obtain constructive criticism at the end of the interview if it is by telephone.

BREAKFAST, LUNCH, AND DINNER INTERVIEWS

An interview over breakfast, lunch, or dinner in a restaurant or private club offers many pitfalls for the unwary. On one hand, it generally means you have passed muster and are being strongly considered for a position. On the other hand, since it gives the interviewer a chance to observe how you behave in a social setting, the risk is that the informality may trip you up more easily than an office interview. Don't make the mistake of thinking this is a social occasion, and drop indiscreet or gossipy statements about your personal life or your former or current employer.

Always remember: the interviewer is not taking you out to eat because he or she likes you and wants to become better acquainted. Everything from your social etiquette, table manners, treatment of staff, to your choice of conversational topics will be scrutinized. If you are interviewing for a position that demands a lot of client contact, your behavior is quite important. Act relaxed, but don't let your guard drop for a moment—follow the lead of your interviewer for cues.

Helpful Tips

1. Avoid any alcohol. This holds true even if your interviewer is drinking up a storm, and coaxing you to do the same. Your mind should remain clear at all times; it's too dangerous to let alcohol ruin your career chances by loosening your tongue or impairing your judgment.

2. Avoid messy or difficult foods. This includes lobster, fried chicken, barbecued dishes, linguine or spaghetti, and finger foods. You don't want a morsel of food shooting across the table and zapping your poise.

3. Do not talk with your mouth full. Basic etiquette is always worth remembering.

4. Do not over-order. If you order gigantic portions, or ask for seconds or thirds, your interviewer will assume you are immoderate in your business habits as well.

5. Do not complain about service, food, or the restaurant. Grousing to the waiter or sending food back will only reflect badly upon the interviewer's choice of setting or possibly send a signal you will be abrasive with subordinates.

6. Do not order the most or least expensive item on the menu. Show you have common sense and a basic understanding of the purpose of your meeting.

7. Do not order highly spiced dishes or food with garlic. You want your breath to remain fresh and sweet.

8. Make sure glasses and cups are far away from the edge of the table. Knocking over a glass or cup will do little for your confidence level. However, if it happens, don't allow it to shatter your poise—remain calm and clean up the spill quickly without missing a beat in your conversation.

9. Do not rest your elbows on the table. Also, sit up straight in your chair.

10. Leave your knife and fork across your plate when you are finished with your meal, so the waitperson will know you are done.

11. Do not offer to share the cost of the meal or even the tip. Even if the waiter gives you the check, rest assured your host's expense account will cover the meal.

12. Do not smoke. If you are a smoker, don't smoke unless your interviewer does. It is best to wait until after dinner to smoke. This is simply common courtesy.

13. Avoid controversial topics. Try to avoid talking about politics, religion, or any other issue which generates strong reactions. If the interviewer brings up a controversial topic, try tactfully to find out his or her opinion before stating yours. If this is not possible, steer a neutral course by making an abstract point about the issue—without blatantly favoring a candidate or viewpoint. If you can

relate the issue at all to your industry or the position you are seeking, do so.

14. Do not pontificate. Your objective is to win the job, not a convert to your point of view.

15. Use "small talk" to your advantage to display some individuality. Mention a hobby or interest which displays traits or skills needed in the job you are seeking. Find some common ground with the interviewer, and share your insights. For example, recommend a favorite vacation spot if your interviewer is seeking suggestions.

STRESS INTERVIEWS

You sit down for the interview, and, after a few innocuous questions, the interviewer starts rapid-firing tough questions and even sardonic rejoinders at you in a hostile, contentious tone. Or maybe the interviewer starts contradicting or challenging almost everything you say and just doesn't let up. You are taken aback and cannot imagine what you have done to offend the interviewer—you are here for a job, not a grilling on your shortcomings—and feel mortified and defensive. You shift uncomfortably in your seat, your heart starts pounding rapidly, and your confidence level plummets. Your responses become mumbled, halting, and stilted—or faster, nervous, and incoherent.

No, the interviewer has not suddenly undergone a transformation from Dr. Jekyll to Mr. Hyde. He or she is simply trying to rattle you to observe how you behave under pressure, a crucial component of many jobs which require dealing with the public or clients in pressure-filled situations. Don't fall into the trap. Don't take it personally, and refuse to be intimidated. You should rise to the challenge and respond like the cool-headed, savvy professional you are. A fatal mistake is to match the interviewer's attitude and become argumentative yourself. Another is to drop unguarded remarks you would have kept to yourself if the interview proceeded in a calmer, more expected fashion.

This interview style, by the way, is akin to the journalistic technique of disarming the subject, then circling in for the kill. One reason it is used so often is that it works—giving interviewers and journalists a realistic sense of their subjects not otherwise obtained through rehearsed answers to predictable questions. Don't be surprised if your tormenter lapses back into his or her cordial self and shakes your hand warmly after your "interrogation." The interviewer was only doing his or her job, trying to test your mettle to see if you are the kind of fast-track, hard-driving individual the company is looking for.

Of course, most interviews feature questions and comments which instill stress—if not downright terror—in the job-seeker. These include the infamous "Tell me about yourself," the dreaded "Why were you fired from your last few positions?" and the tricky "What didn't you like about your previous employer?" The best way to combat such stress is to anticipate these questions, and prepare thoroughly, so that answering them becomes second-nature. These questions, and suggested responses, are covered at length in Chapter 6. Illegal questions are covered in Chapter 7.

GROUP INTERVIEWS

Interviews by a group of people—a boss and some subordinates, or two or three partners or executives of equal rank—are becoming more and more popular. This is particularly true if the company employs a team approach and wants to involve several key executives in the hiring process to see if the job applicant will fit into the team—and save time. So be prepared. Group interviews are usually stressful, with questions shooting at you right and left, disrupting your concentration. It's difficult trying to focus on the interviewer and read his or her reactions to your responses to questions, the way one can in a one-on-one interview. Some anxious job-seekers compare group interviews to going before a firing squad.

The best approach is to remain calm and collected. Focus on one question and one interviewer at a time, as though he or she were the only person in the room. Don't let the group situation "rattle" you. Pause after a question, or use a stalling technique such as repeating the question, or using a filler like "let me give you an example"—if you start to feel distracted. Don't let the group reduce you to a puddle of passivity either. Feel free to ask questions, make your two-minute "pitch" and any other points you set out to make—just the way you would in a one-on-one interview. If one interviewer interrupts you mid-sentence while you are answering another interviewer's question, refuse to be rattled. Finish the first question calmly and fully, then turn to the interviewer addressing the second question and answer that. You can always say something like, "I'll be happy to answer that question, but first let me give an example of how I managed to increase sales during my first year at Company X."

Being interviewed with a group of other job-seekers means you are being tested on your interpersonal, leadership, and negotiating skills. Often, the interviewer proposes a situation or problem, which the group is asked to reach an agreement on.

TELEPHONE INTERVIEWS

See the telephone interview for what it is: less a telephone call than a mini-sales presentation.

A telephone interview can result from several sources:

- your telephone call to an employer in response to an ad or an article you read
- your telephone call to a networking contact
- your telephone call to a lead referred by a networking contact
- your telephone call to an executive recruiter
- a telephone call from an employer in response to your résumé
- an appointment arranged by you or by an executive recruiter

Regardless of how a telephone interview is generated, always be prepared. Keep your résumé, and information on the company you are calling (or expect a call from), near the telephone for easy reference. If the call is a surprise—let's say you are in the shower, a child is crying, or you have just walked in the door—ask the caller to hold on a moment. Then, collect your thoughts, take a few deep breaths to calm yourself, and assemble your résumé and other materials.

Since the call is a sales pitch, immediately get to the point if you are making the call. Introduce yourself, mention the name of your referral source or the ad or article spurring the call, and cite reasons why your qualifications are suitable for the job in question. Be brief, cogent, and, after a short give-and-take of questions from both yourself and the other person, ask for a face-to-face interview.

Remember to take notes, which will help you bone up for the interview.

Executive recruiter Elisabeth Ryan, vice president at Heyman Associates, a search firm which specializes in placing public relations executives, recommends these do's and don'ts on telephone etiquette:

DO'S

Research the company, contact, or executive recruiter. Find out about the executive or recruiter you're calling. A commonality of interests or background creates immediate rapport—plus people are impressed that you've made the effort. For example, one candidate learned that the recruiter he was calling was an avid sports fan so he played up the fact that he had written several sports books.

Identify someone you can use as a recommendation. It helps to have a mutual acquaintance, one you are confident is well-respected by the person you are calling. Just make sure your contact really knows who you are and will say nice things.

Make the person you're calling feel good. Everyone likes to be praised. Telling an executive that you heard she was a great boss, or a recruiter that he's the person that really knows the industry, can help your cause.

Cut to the chase. Most executives and recruiters don't have the time to schmooze. Get to the point of your call and explain why you think you are an attractive candidate. Start by asking if this is a good time to talk and, if not, find out when he or she is available.

Sound professional and upbeat. Don't call back excessively—there is a thin line between being persistent and becoming a nuisance. Don't call from a pay phone if trains are rumbling in the background, or from home if you're competing with kids screaming or dogs barking. If you're beeped or the other phone rings, don't put your caller on hold to answer it. When leaving a message, be succinct.

Handle callbacks appropriately. Thank callers for getting back to you. Do not have a cutesy or unprofessional message on your answering machine.

DON'TS

Whine about your past or present job or boss. No one wants to hear anyone who starts out by saying "I hate my job" or "I haven't gotten a raise in two years."

Sound desperate or beg. An air of desperation makes most people tune out. Always sound confident of yourself and your abilities.

Assume because you sent in your résumé anyone's read it. Be prepared to start from the beginning.

Call without thinking about what you're going to say. This goes back to the premise that your contact does not have a lot of time to waste. Plan a general script and stick to it.

Call Monday mornings. This is when most people play catch-up and won't want any unnecessary interruptions. Friday afternoon is usually a good time: people are looking forward to the weekend and in a better mood to talk. A good strategy is to call before 9:00 A.M. or after 5:00 P.M. You are less likely to interrupt a person during the heat of the workday, and less apt to encounter overprotective secretaries.

If, for any reason, you fail to show up for an interview—and do not call to reschedule—Ms. Ryan notes: "You're done. People call me months later, in the hopes that I've forgotten. Believe me, you don't forget."

PRE-INTERVIEW STRATEGIES

There are a number of strategies, both long-range and short-term, you can employ to create the most favorable impression so the odds will be stacked in your favor on a job interview. Call them the five P's— preparation, practice, positive thinking, punctuality, and politeness. Approaching an interview without heeding these tactics is like going into battle unarmed. Follow each one diligently, and you will automatically be head and shoulders above much of your competition.

1. PREPARATION

Nothing turns an interviewer off more than a job-seeker who clearly is not informed about the company. Research the company, industry, and even the interviewer thoroughly using the techniques described in Chapter 1. Use directories, annual reports, and other public relations materials, articles in newspapers, business and trade magazines, and talk to people who know the company. Know the company's size, position in the industry, product lines or services, potential products and services, competition, current trends, organizational structure, career path in your field, challenges, and problems. Pretend you're back in school cramming for an exam or playing a game to win. Do whatever it takes to get your competitive juices flowing. It's best to read first, then talk to informed sources later, so your questions will be sharper and more intelligent. Knowledge is an unbeatable tool on an interview. It'll knock the socks off your interviewer, lessen your anxiety, and automatically disqualify lazier job-seekers who can't hold a candle to you.

"The more powerful and knowledgeable you feel, the better you'll do in an interview," says Kate Wendleton, founder of The Five O'Clock Club. "You're more apt to take control, and not be reactive. Often, when you need this feeling the most, you have it the least."

In addition to long-term preparation, carefully select the materials you will bring to the interview. This should include several résumé— the interviewer may have misplaced yours or may want to pass it on to colleagues—pad of paper, two pens (to take notes during the interview), business cards, and letters of reference and/or other evidence of your accomplishments. Bring a portfolio of your work if you are in a field, such as public relations, advertising, or graphic design, which requires it. Be sure everything is neat, crisp, and up-to-date to create the best possible impression. Carry everything in an attractive, new-looking leather briefcase. Substance may be more important than style in the long run—but in a job interview, aim for both. You want to present yourself as a competent, organized professional with mastery over your domain.

Plan what you will wear on your interview the night before, and scrutinize details carefully. Make sure your clothing is spotlessly clean and fresh. Fix loose buttons and sagging hems. Shoes should be polished, and the heels should not be worn down. Women should bring an extra pair of pantyhose—it's embarrassing trying to conceal an unsightly run or hole in a stocking during a job interview. More specific information about dressing for an interview has been covered in Chapter 3.

Get a full night's sleep the night before. Your appearance will suffer, and sleep deprivation generally depresses your energy level and alertness. If you think pre-interview jitters will prevent you from falling asleep, strenuous exercise—running, jogging, a session at the gym—should help. Finish up with a warm bath or shower to relax your muscles, and perhaps a glass of milk.

2. PRACTICE

Remember the cliché about how to get to Carnegie Hall: practice. Interviewing is a skill, just like playing the piano or playing baseball—the more you do it, the better you get. Rehearse the questions you expect will be asked during the interview and your responses—as well as those you don't expect—and questions you intend to ask. Practicing in front of a mirror—noting if you look calm and unruffled or tense and frowning—with an audiocassette recorder is very helpful. Or borrow a tactic from top corporate executives and videotape your presentation, then review for improvement.

If you can convince a friend or spouse to play the role of interviewer, so much the better. But ask for an honest, unvarnished opinion—do you come across as arrogant, nervous, or overly humble? Is your voice too high-pitched? Are you talking too fast? This is the only way you'll learn. The aim of these exercises, of course, is to diminish your fear of the unexpected so you'll feel confident and familiar with the interview process.

Write the following key points on an index card. Review them at regular intervals. Most importantly, refer to them just before you walk into a job interview.

- What is your "two-minute pitch"?
- Why should this company should hire you?
- Name a few achievements or examples to back up your suitability for the position.
- What are the questions you hope the interviewer won't ask? What are your answers to them?

Review your résumé beforehand and practice answering questions about it—a two-year gap in employment, many years in the same position, a technical specialty of yours, etc. Even if your résumé was professionally prepared, you have no excuse for not knowing its content.

Consider each interview as a learning experience and as practice for the next. Never think of one interview as the be-all and end-all. Correct any mistakes with the next interview. It is always best to schedule really "important" interviews after you have passed the hurdles with interviews that interest you less. A good piece of advice is to accept all interviews that come your way—since you never know when you will meet someone or uncover a nugget of information that may help in your job search.

3. POSITIVE ATTITUDE

Harness the power of your mind so it works for you, not against you. Think positively throughout your job search but in particular the night before and the day of your interview. Repeat confidence-building affirmations such as "I'm going to be a success in this interview" to yourself until they stick. Try visualizing a positive interview outcome by filling in as many details as possible. Watch yourself walk in and smile at the interviewer, answer questions confidently and competently, and feel your triumph as you are offered the job at an excellent salary. Read a few articles or skim through books that promote positive thinking. *Think and Grow Rich* by Napoleon Hill (less materialistic than it sounds), *The Power of Positive Thinking* by Norman Vincent Peale, and *The Magic of Believing* by Claude Bristol are good choices. Let them fill you with a warm glow of can-do optimism.

Just before your interview, take several deep breaths, and feel anxiety and doubts drain from your body. Sit erect, shoulders back, and notice how you seem more confident. Feel calm, relaxed, and centered, not scattered.

4. PUNCTUALITY

One key to feeling calm and relaxed is arriving on time for your interview. Check the address, directions, and the amount of travel time carefully before the interview date. It might even be a good idea to do a trial run and scout out the location ahead of time. Don't run the risk of arriving at West 57th Street when you're supposed to be across town at East 57th Street. Dashing breathlessly into your interview distraught because you couldn't get a taxi is not a good way to begin. The best tactic is to arrive at the building early. You can then compose yourself in the lobby, waiting room, or coffee shop and freshen up in the restroom before your meeting. If you are late, make a brief apology but appear calm and unruffled—don't let this ruin the interview. If it looks like you are going to be quite late, call ahead and state the reason—the train was late, an accident delayed traffic, etc. Of course, avoid unnecessarily long and painful details.

5. POLITENESS

Be sure you are polite to everyone you encounter at the company before your job interview—the receptionist, secretary, etc. You may be surprised how their opinions may be relayed to high places.

HOW TO READ THE INTERVIEWER

A job-seeker sometimes returns from an interview convinced he or she has "nailed it." "He loved me," the applicant exults to the recruiter. "He was ready to offer me the job right then and there."

Later, however, the recruiter gets the real story from the client. Not only was the interviewer not terribly impressed—the job-seeker is not even in the running as a candidate.

How did he or she so misinterpret the manner of the interviewer? And can he or she learn to read signals more accurately—and perhaps even change the interviewer's impression midstream?

"A job-seeker must recognize the difference between an interviewer acting politely and showing genuine interest," says Bill Heyman, president of Heyman Associates, an executive search firm specializing in the public relations field. "Most people are nice at such meetings, hesitant to be negative or confrontational with a stranger. Rarely will an interviewer come out and tell a candidate he or she is not right for the job."

While some people adopt a poker face which makes them all but impossible to read, a perceptive job-seeker can learn to sense the true interest (or lack thereof) of most interviewers—and respond appropriately.

The first clue to size up is the interviewer's office, which may help the job-seeker understand his or her personality or decide whether this is the type of person who would be desirable as a boss. An office devoid of any personal or family photos, for example, would tend to belong to either a no-nonsense or private type (or someone with no life outside the office). An elaborate filing system and workbooks that are color-coded, in alphabetical order, and neatly aligned on the shelves would likely signify a highly organized and detail-oriented person. The occupant of an office full of photos of himself in the company of celebrities and politicians probably takes himself fairly seriously.

Mr. Heyman recommends the following tips to spot trouble signals in an interview, and how to turn things around:

> The interviewer suddenly adopts a chatty tone that has nothing to do with a discussion of the job or your qualifications for it. When he or she starts to discuss an upcoming vacation or a new-found love for a hobby, it usually means the interviewer no longer takes you seriously. Refocus attention on the job itself and why you are suitable.

> The interviewer seems anxious to end the interview. The length of an interview is directly related to the interviewer's interest level. Don't be fooled into thinking otherwise. In today's job market, few people are hired for any meaningful job or advanced to the next round of interviews after a 5- or 10-minute interview. Ask questions to sustain interest in you.

> The interviewer's questions seem scattered. This probably means your answers are not sufficient to hold his or her attention. Re-evaluate what you've said and anticipate the kind of answers the interviewer expects.

> The interviewer's body language indicates that he or she is pulling away or is becoming impatient. A perceptive person can tell when someone is turned on or off by reading his or her body language. Is the interviewer pushing away from the desk? Or checking a watch? Or unable to sustain eye contact? Is he or she looking for help from a secretary? You can confront the issue by asking if the interviewer is late for an appointment and would like to reschedule.

> The interviewer informs you that you are one of many intervie-wees with excellent credentials. Translation: Don't feel bad you're

not getting the job. Rise to the challenge and convince him or her you are the one.

The interviewer seems particularly lethargic. This may be his or her personality, boredom with you, or merely the fact that you are the twenty-fourth interview of the day. Wake the interviewer up—take charge and show enthusiasm.

The interviewer ends by thanking you for your time. If he or she ends the interview without noting another step in the process—a second interview, the suggestion of a test, meeting someone else—the party is over. You can be assertive and ask about the next step, but you'll probably get an answer like "Someone will get back to you." Evaluate what went amiss, and be better prepared for the next interview.

CHAPTER FIVE

The Art of an Interview

PROMOTING YOUR ABILITIES

P ut all emotion aside when preparing for job interviews. Your professional abilities, not your personal needs, are being assessed. Never make the mistake of assuming you'll be hired because you need a job. You'll be hired only if the *employer needs you*—and thinks you will help the company reach its goals.

Always accept this cold, harsh reality of a job interview. The priority for the interviewer is to hire someone with specific qualifications, and methodically winnow out all job-seekers who do not match the profile of the ideal candidate. Understanding the mind-set of the interviewer will make a powerful difference in conducting your interviews successfully so they will lead to job offers. Think and act like a consultant or colleague who can make a genuine contribution in solving specific problems the company faces. To paraphrase the late John F. Kennedy's famous maxim: "Ask not what the interviewer can do for you, but what you can do for the interviewer."

"Part of being a good interview is demonstrating the same skills that help you on the job," says Dale Winston, president of Battalia Winston International, an executive search firm. "Corporations are looking for people who are succinct, clearly define what their roles were in their companies, what the challenges were, and what significant contributions they made to their functions or the business as a whole."

Another serious mistake is thinking an interview is an introductory chat to meet you and ask a few questions about your résumé. Don't be fooled. Job interviews are sales calls, but a unique sort—you are the salesperson as well as the product. Your message should be finely honed, highlighting all your positive personality traits, skills, and achievements—and systematically overcoming any objections. In Chapter 6, you will find 100 tough questions and suggested responses to help you.

Like any salesperson, you should become accustomed to rejection, and accept it as a natural part of the process. Don't take it personally—view it as a learning experience, which points up elements in your message that need refining. Job interviews, like many things in life, are a numbers game. The more you participate, the better your chances of winning.

"Fear of rejection is the single biggest obstacle to getting a job," says résumé and job counseling expert Stanley Wynett. "Instead of fearing or avoiding interviews, realize the reason you're invited in is because you're a hot property—so act accordingly."

PROVING YOU ARE THE BEST CANDIDATE

Unfortunately, qualifications are not the be-all and end-all in a job interview today. In this ultracompetitive, lean and mean market, companies may interview dozens of highly qualified applicants for a job, ask more probing questions than a therapist, and invite a chosen few to return for repeated interviews. Blind faith that your substance will win over another's style is ill-advised. Presentation is all-important, but luckily it is a learned skill. The secret to winning job offers is to *prove* you can do the job and fit into the company—before you get the job. The trick is to explain your ability clearly and compellingly, in terms of your experience and background, so the interviewer is as convinced as you are.

How do you do this? Take out a piece of paper and draw up a comprehensive list of your skills, achievements, and personality traits. Stack them up against the requirements of the job you are seeking. (See the example below.) Then, think up examples or anecdotes which illustrate each of your strengths. Be prepared to describe them in a lively but brief fashion in your interviews, and weave them seamlessly into questions posed by the interviewer.

Giving examples and anecdotes to back up your strengths is key to making a strong case that you are the one for the job. The examples help paint a vivid picture—so that the interviewer can actually visualize you demonstrating a positive trait or excellent performance in your old job. Just mouthing phrases like "I am reliable" or "I am goal-oriented and work well under pressure" will not convince anyone. Think of how newspaper or magazine stories grab your attention and make you care about an issue through the creative use of examples. A story on poor families in the inner city features a 23-year-old single mother with two children struggling to survive on a meager public assistance check, and her hopes and fears for the future. A program that helps small businesses grow comes alive with the success story of a college dropout and

JOB SKILLS REQUIREMENTS MATCH

Job Title: _Director Community Relations_   Name of Company: _Wilton Memorial Hospital_

Job Requirement	My Qualifications	Proof
5-10 years' experience in medical public relations	eight years' experience—worked as hospital PR director	PR Director Brookside Hospital, 1986-1993
excellent media/press contacts	for six years in a PR agency handling pharmaceutical accounts	Senior Account Executive, LMK Public Relations, 1993-1995

artist who started a home-based graphic design business which now employs four people and has revenues of $1 million.

Let's take this indispensable trio—personality traits, skills, and achievements—one by one.

PERSONALITY TRAITS EMPLOYERS LOOK FOR IN JOB APPLICANTS

According to a survey by career experts, good verbal communication ranks highest on the list of what impresses prospective employers most in job interviews. Other desirable qualities include enthusiasm, a neat and well-groomed appearance, honesty, experience, confidence, a sense of humor, and preparedness.

Attitude and verbal communication skills were also tops in a 1994 U.S. Census Bureau survey of what 3,000 employers found most important in hiring non-supervisory or production workers. Previous work experience ranked third, recommendations from current and previous employers ranked fourth and fifth, while teacher recommendations ranked lowest in the list of 11 factors.

Key personality traits employers desire are:

1. Problem-solving/analytical ability—Can you zero in on a difficult situation, evaluate the pros and cons objectively, and resolve the problem? If you view a job in light of the problems and challenges it presents, you are more apt to convince an employer you are capable of handling the job.
2. Intelligence—Being knowledgeable enough to perform the job combined with street smarts and a healthy dose of common sense.
3. Enthusiasm—Passion or zeal for the job is crucial, otherwise technical proficiency counts for little. An employee with a burning desire to do the job will go that extra mile and make things happen.
4. Team player—Being able to cooperate with others as part of a team, sharing information and credit. Being willing to be managed by your supervisor. Employers generally find "lone wolves" difficult and unpredictable.
5. Honesty—Trustworthiness is crucial. Employees with integrity, who are straightforward in their dealings and have the company's best interests at heart, are worth their weight in gold.
6. Reliability—Being able to be counted upon to get the job done—and done well—on a regular basis with minimal supervision.

7. Drive—Being motivated to achieve the goals set by yourself or others, to get the job done and excel no matter what.

8. Energy—A high energy level enabling an employee to tackle each day's projects with vigor is desirable.

9. Good communication skills—Being able to talk, write, and listen effectively to people within and outside the company is now more crucial than ever.

10. Dedication—The ability to exert effort, stay the course, and put in long hours if necessary to complete projects on deadline.

11. Determination—Resoluteness of purpose without being deterred by obstacles.

12. Flexibility—Having the ability to cope with change and go with the flow.

13. Results-Oriented—Taking the initiative to get things accomplished.

14. Self-Awareness—Knowing your strengths and weaknesses as well as making a good appearance.

SELLING YOUR STRENGTHS, ACHIEVEMENTS, AND SKILLS

"The six most beautiful words in the English language you can say to a prospective employer are 'I will never let you down,'" says Mr. Wynett, who also contributes to the *National Business Employment Weekly*. Other statements that are music to an interviewer's ears, Mr. Wynett notes, are:

"I work until the job is done."

"I'm willing to make sacrifices to get results."

"I'm easy to train."

"I want to help you cut expenses."

"I never miss a deadline."

"I want this job and know I can handle it to your complete satisfaction; just give me the chance to prove myself."

Of course, just mouthing phrases like "I am reliable" or "I am goal-oriented and work well under pressure" is not enough to woo a seasoned interviewer. This is where your thoughtfully crafted examples come in to prove your point. For example, mention the time your commuter train was on strike for a week—yet you drove to work, leaving home every day at 6:00 A.M. to complete your project on time and make up for staffers who missed work. Or the time you worked from 8:00 A.M. to midnight six days a week for almost two months because of a big merger deal.

PROMOTE YOUR ACHIEVEMENTS

Carefully analyze your job history in terms of accomplishments. What activities and measurable achievements can you point to with pride where you helped your company achieve such goals as increasing profits, lowering expenses, or developing new products? All dollar figures or numbers make an interviewer sit up and take notice. Again, be prepared to explain *how* you achieved your goals.

You need not be an executive or professional to cite achievements. All support staff make contributions to a company's success. Individual initiative is what's important—how you performed your job differently from others with the same position.

Let's look at a few sample achievements:

- As regional manager, I increased sales 22 percent last year in the computer software division.
- In my position as senior buyer, I saved my company over $200,000 in purchasing office supplies by changing vendors and negotiating a new contract.
- During the last six months, I brought in three new clients with combined annual billings of $250,000.
- As office manager, I supervised the training and work of 10 administrative assistants.
- As copywriter on an ad campaign introducing a new deluxe hotel, I contributed to the booking of 10,000 rooms in the first three months.
- In my human resources position, I decreased employee turnover 7 percent over a two-year period due to incentive programs I initiated.
- As an administrative assistant, I automated 12,000 handwritten medical records.
- As technical writer, I produced and edited the company's new training manual on networking services.
- As project manager, I supervised the construction of a new 12-story office building, which was completed two days early with no extra cost to the developer.

DEMONSTRATE YOUR SKILLS

The following are some skills you may possess. Be prepared to discuss them in greater detail. (See Chapter 2 on résumés for a comprehensive list of skills.)

- computer proficiency (knowledge of specific spreadsheet, database, or word processing programs)
- fluency in foreign languages
- writing advertising and promotional copy
- supervisory or management skills
- knowledge of accounting or finance
- sales or marketing background
- speaking to groups
- specialized knowledge or technical background
- teaching or tutoring

CONVERSATIONAL STYLE

Be as proactive as possible in an interview, asking intelligent and alert questions. View the situation as a two-way process, with a give-and-take between the parties. You are there to learn more about the job and its requirements to see if it interests you. The interviewer is there to learn more about you, not to be an interrogator.

Always keep the conversational ball rolling: Don't answer questions with just "yes" or "no," or utter meaningless clichés ("I love the entertainment field," "I'm a people person"). Respond to questions fully but cogently—speak no longer than two minutes at a time. When finished, note how the interviewer responds. If he or she asks you to elaborate or looks interested, add more details; if he or she says nothing or looks bored, stay silent until another question is asked. Remember, the best interviews produce genuine dialogue on how the candidate can contribute to the company.

If a question seems too open-ended for you or if you are not sure what the interviewer wants to know, ask for a little more definition to frame the question. The interviewer will almost always oblige. Let's say "Tell me about yourself" gives you the jitters—ask if the interviewer wants to hear about any specific aspect of your work history or skills before launching into a monologue.

Stalling can be used if you want a few moments' grace to formulate a response. Ask the interviewer to repeat the question while you think about what you plan to say. Or say, "That's a good question. I'd like to think about that a minute or two." Don't think you need to blurt out a response in record time whenever you are asked a question. Reflection and good judgment are desirable traits in the corporate world.

LEARN FROM THE PROS

Follow the lead from politicians in your interview style. These master communicators—who otherwise would not win elections—rarely miss a chance to get their points across in a TV, radio, or newspaper interview, regardless of the questions asked. This applies even if the questions posed are hostile! Do the same. Tell the interviewer about your achievements by weaving them into your responses even if you are not specifically asked. Say "This reminds me of when I headed a quality control team at my company and we succeeded in shaving production costs 12%," or "Yes, I am used to working in a high-pressure environment. I thrive at it—at my last PR agency I handled eight clients alone under tight deadline pressure while supervising several people."

One technique politicians and others accustomed to dealing with journalists use often is called speaking in "sound bites." These are short, pithy, information-packed sentences of no more than a minute or two, particularly common in TV and radio interviews.

Another journalistic technique can also help you: communicating in "pyramid" style. Journalistic rules demand that a hard-news story be written with a first paragraph that summarizes the most important information up front, later paragraphs with lead sentences that briefly describe the contents, and minor details toward the end so the story can be cut easily. Conversationally, this means you should open a response to a question with a brief summary statement. The interviewer can always ask you to sketch in more details if he or she wants. This way, you do not risk boring your interviewer with a long, rambling tale that begins at the very beginning and eventually winds up with a point that, unfortunately, the interviewer misses.

If you have a negative or difficult situation to explain, it's best to acknowledge your mistake or a bad situation with grace and confidence. Particularly in more senior positions, how one handles a situation is more important than the situation itself. This applies regardless of whether your company has downsized 10,000 people and you are a casualty, your career has been marked by hopscotching from job to job, your law practice has dwindled to almost nothing since your industry specialty has fallen upon hard times, there is a lengthy gap in your work history, or the interviewer knows you have been fired.

"A lot of interview candidates shoot themselves in the foot by apologizing and overexplaining. They get a little flustered, and start talking in painful detail about things better left unsaid—it's very revealing," says Richard Linde, vice president at Battalia Winston International.

At the end of the interview, summarize your qualifications in a neat package. Say something like: "I am very interested in the job. I believe the combination of my experience in opening up Eastern European markets in my last job, my 10 years marketing a very similar product, and my fluency in German make me a good fit for the job."

HOW TO OVERCOME OBJECTIONS

It's tempting, when an interviewer voices an objection such as "You seem overqualified for us," "It looks like you've jumped around a lot in your career," or "Your experience in this area seems a little light," to think he or she doesn't want to hire you, or that the interview is heading downhill fast. It's easy for you to feel defensive and confrontational, perhaps raise your voice, or blurt out an unrehearsed remark—and, ironically, blow your chances for a job offer.

Far better to view an objection for what it is: a sales opportunity. The interviewer has just handed you a chance to prove your mettle. Like a seasoned salesperson, you should treat an objection as a challenge—anticipate it, understand the rationale behind it, and prepare a compelling response which shows you (the product) are the best thing in the world for the employer (the customer). It's often a good idea to let the interviewer know that you know "where he or she is coming from," by prefacing your response with something like "I understand your concern," or "I'd like to address that."

Let's look at some objections which may be raised one by one, and develop appropriate responses.

IF YOU ARE OVERQUALIFIED

Interviewers may be concerned if you are overqualified because:

- you will be bored and frustrated since the job is below your capabilities, and you won't last long before looking for another job more in tune with your skills
- you are willing to take a substantial cut in salary, which makes the employer worry why you are available at "fire sale" prices

- you will demand a high salary that matches or is above your current salary, and so are too expensive
- your superior achievements and skills threaten the manager, who fears you will be gunning for his or her job
- your experience and skills will make you want to "take over" the department or company
- you are "too old"—they prefer someone younger and on the way up

If the interviewer thinks your superior record of achievements or high educational level will doom you to boredom, wishing for greener pastures, your goal is to convince him or her that you fulfill the job requirements and the job is exactly right for you at this time in your life. For example, you maybe seeking a job in a public relations agency after heading your own home-based PR agency for several years. The employer may worry you will miss running your own show, will balk at taking direction, and will not cooperate or share information for a smooth-running team. Argue that you really crave a stable job with benefits and holidays off, and will not miss the headaches and pressure of bringing in new clients or the round-the-clock pace.

Or it may be necessary to explain what your advanced degree or previous work experience really means, and demonstrate practical applications of your knowledge and specific problems solved. Employers often have the perception that a Ph.D., working in a think tank or teaching at a university, harbors an ivory tower mentality and is hopelessly out of touch with the gritty realities of the business world.

One solution is to "dequalify" yourself, and delete from your résumé and interview high-level achievements, doctorates, law degrees, etc., which may put you out of the running. Some applicants use several different résumés, including a "neutral" one which deletes or downplays these facts.

If age is the problem—and the "overqualification" charge simply masks this—highlight your many years of experience and managerial strengths. Of course, age discrimination is illegal, but most interviewers will not come out and blatantly state the problem. (See Chapter 10 on how to overcome negative stereotypes of older people.)

If salary is the bugaboo—the interviewer is suspicious as to why you're willing to take such a cut in pay—reassure him or her that this job is the perfect fit for your qualifications, and meshes with your career aspirations at this time: concerns that are more important to you than salary. If your current salary is too high, reassure the interviewer that money will not be a problem—you are flexible, and prefer to hear more about the job itself. Hopefully, you have not raised the salary issue—a no-no—but the interviewer has. (See Chapters 6 and 9 for specific approaches to handling salary questions.)

IF YOU LACK EXPERIENCE

If you lack specific experience for the job, demonstrate transferable skills from your current or previous job—even if it is in a different industry—volunteer work, internships, college, or extracurricular activities. In addition—or if this is not possible—show you are a quick and eager learner. As discussed, enthusiasm is one of the most highly rated traits by employers, and can compensate for a multitude of sins. Be willing to go the extra mile—offer to write a business plan or think up some creative ideas to prove you can do the job, instead of passively waiting, hoping the interviewer will take a chance on you.

Kate Wendleton, founder of The Five O'Clock Club, tells the story of a woman, a former lobbyist, who applied for a position at a law firm. She was told the law firm also needed some public relations work and an internal newsletter produced—two areas in which she had no experience. Instead of just expressing confidence that she could fulfill both tasks if hired, she decided to take the initiative and leave no doubt in the interviewer's mind that she was capable of doing the job. She wrote a PR plan—after borrowing sample plans from other people—obtained copies of newsletters from other law firms, and then wrote a strong thank you note stating she would be happy to review the plan. The result? She won the job.

A lot of work, you may counter—but so are repeated job interviews.

IF YOU HAVE A SPOTTY WORK HISTORY

Periods of unemployment and a series of jobs are much more common than they ever were. Explain with poise and confidence, without a trace of defensiveness, how you occupied yourself productively during gaps between jobs—consulting assignments, taking classes, volunteer work, helping out in your son's business, etc. If you are a job-hopper, mention any transferable skills, praise the vast experience, and explain how everything until now has prepared you for this job, where your qualifications match the requirements. Steer the conversation away from the past and toward the future, where you can make a solid contribution.

QUESTIONS TO ASK THE INTERVIEWER

Asking the interviewer questions demonstrates several things:

- How knowledgeable and up-to-date you are about the company.
- How proactive and self-starting you are—desirable traits in many positions.
- What the position involves and what kind of person the interviewer is looking for—clues you can use to prove you are the right candidate.
- How the interviewer thinks—clues you can use to your advantage in selling yourself.
- If the position will interest you.

The following are questions you may want to ask the interviewer:

What are the major responsibilities of this position?

Where does this position fit into the corporate structure?

How is the department organized?

What will be the first projects you expect to be tackled?

What is a typical path for career advancement in your company?

What kinds of people get promoted?

Who will be the supervisor?

Can I meet the supervisor?

What is the management style used by the supervisor?

Are there specific clients or customers you expect your new employee to handle?

What is the work environment like day-to-day?

Why is the position open?

Why is the position being filled from the outside?

How long has the position been open?

What happened to the employee who previously held the position?

Does the company plan to expand or pursue a new direction for future growth over the next few years?

How many people will I supervise, and what are their backgrounds?

Are there any aspects of my background or skills you would like to hear more about?

Is there a management training program?

Are there other educational opportunities available for employees?

Who has the final say in the hiring decision?

Can I meet some of the people I would be working with?

What strategy did the company use to increase its market share so dramatically last year?

Is there anything else I should know about this company?

JOB INTERVIEW GUIDELINES

DO'S

DO your homework. If there's one thing interviewers are unanimously eager about, it's job-seekers who demonstrate knowledge and insightfulness about the company and its position in the industry.

DO express enthusiasm, energy, and excitement about the prospective job.

DO get the interviewer to like you. Some job experts claim the hiring decision is 100 percent emotional. Others believe it is mainly emotional, with a pinch of logic mixed in. At any rate, be pleasant, smile, make a comment about a mutual interest.

DO pay attention to cues (verbal and nonverbal) from the interviewer.

DO show integrity and sincerity, which inspire trust.

DO summarize often. Make brief summary statements, then fill in further details, and close the interview with a summary of your qualifications and interest in the job.

DO display a sense of humor. Don't take yourself too seriously.

DO build your achievements, personality traits, and skills into answers to questions.

DO use examples to illustrate your achievements, personality traits, and skills.

DON'TS

DON'T say that if you are not promoted, you will be unhappy.

DON'T say you are willing to take this job because of its future. The company is looking for someone to deal with its present needs.

DON'T lie—about anything. This includes salary. Many people have lost prospective jobs because untruths were detected when their work histories were checked.

DON'T answer questions with "yes" or "no." Explain a bit.

DON'T convey the sense that you don't care what you do, as long as you make a lot of money.

DON'T say "in all candor" or "candidly, Jim." This raises questions about your credibility in the rest of the interview, and also "red flags" the interviewer to listen closely—the following statement is often a lie.

DON'T ever badmouth your current employer (or ex-employer). You can either only mention positive things, or find a tactful way to explain a reason for leaving. Don't fall for any bait the interviewer may hand you, such as "tough company you're working for."

DON'T be late. If you are unavoidably late, make a brief, sincere apology, then proceed with the interview.

DON'T use weak, waffling words like "maybe," "I think so," and "kind of." They convey indecisiveness, and raise doubts in the interviewer's mind about how effective you will be as an employee. Project an image of assertiveness and strength.

DON'T ramble or "spill." Talking too much often results in making overly personal remarks, excuses, and endless explanations you would be better off keeping to yourself. Don't be afraid of pauses and brief silences: use them to reflect on what the interviewer has just said and what you plan to say next.

DON'T apologize for your qualifications. Even if you think the company tends to hire people who are younger, older, from Ivy League colleges, or different backgrounds from your own, don't say "I know you usually hire people who are (whatever), but . . . ." Let your qualifications and skills stand on their own.

DON'T argue with the interviewer—about anything. This includes what you have heard about the job versus what the interviewer says.

DON'T re-arrange the furniture so your chair is right next to the interviewer. (It's happened.)

DON'T interrupt the interviewer—or point out he or she is wrong. The interviewer will not thank you if you rush in to finish or restate a thought, or correct a fact or mispronunciation of a word. If he or she misstates a fact in your background or experience, however, politely advise him or her of the truth.

HOW TO COPE WITH STRESS

There's no doubt about it: interviews can be stressful, and repeated rounds of interviewing at many different employers can cause painful feelings of rejection and anxiety for many people. The wrong response, however, is to avoid interviews or go on as few as possible—as a way of minimizing your discomfort. This will help neither your career nor your wallet in the long run—even worse, it may increase the length of your unemployment and cause you to sink into a state of misery.

Dr. Paul J. Rosch, president of The American Institute of Stress and clinical professor of medicine and psychiatry at New York Medical College, offers the following advice to help job-seekers cope with stress and rejection on job interviews:

- Stress is difficult to define because it is different for each of us. Some people may, believe it or not, regard interviewing as an exhilarating experience, and welcome each new interview as a learning experience that brings them one step closer to the job of their dreams. For many others, however, it is a trial to be endured, which can result in physical and psychological symptoms, such as sweating, fidgeting, stammering, insomnia, or overreaction to minor annoyances.

- Stress is an unavoidable consequence of life, but it is important to distinguish between sources of stress we can do something about and others that are inescapable. Like it or not, job interviewing is unavoidable if you are unemployed and want a job, are employed and desire something better. Accept this and realize interviewing need not be a source of stress.

- The most important thing you can learn about stress is to recognize that often it is not external events that are stressful, but rather how you perceive them. Change your mental attitude about job interviews—see them as a game, see yourself as a salesperson where each sales call moves you closer to a "yes." Don't take rejection on a job interview (or 10 interviews) personally and as an attack on your self-worth, and you will be surprised how stressful feelings will diminish.

- Stress is often something that is entirely under your control. Nobody can make you feel inferior without your consent. Thus, you should increase your sense of control over the interview and your confidence by preparing for interview questions, researching the company and industry, making certain your appearance and dress are in tip-top shape, behaving pro-actively, and allowing enough time to arrive at the interview punctually. Since the feeling of being out of control is always stressful, instead of complaining, worrying, and suffering about going on interviews, do all you can to feel "in control" both before and during interviews.

- Stress affects us in different ways. Many techniques can reduce the annoying physical and psychological effects of stress, such as meditation, progressive relaxation, aerobic exercise, jogging, yoga, working out, brisk walks, etc. No technique works for everyone—experiment and find out which is best for you.

- A strong social support system is a powerful stress buffer. If family, friends, or work fail to satisfy this need, join group activities where you meet others with similar interests—such as a job search group, volunteer work, hobby, etc. Doing an activity that benefits others can be very helpful. Feeling adrift in the universe and cut off from human contact will only increase stress.

- Manage your time effectively to allow for sufficient sleep, recreation, and relaxation. If you are unemployed, job-hunting should be a full-time job. You should explore all possibilities, and not give up easily—limiting yourself to "help wanted" ads is a no-win proposition. So is waking up too late, pretending you are on vacation, and slipping into a sloppy, lazy state where you stop shaving, never dress up, etc. These things affect your mood as well as your telephone behavior.

- Establish some appropriate goals that allow you to more fully utilize your talents, and which are within your reach. Unrealistic goals will only lead to chronic frustration, while minor achievements will rob you of the powerful stress-reducing benefits that derive from pride of accomplishment. Resolve to contact a specific number of people, send out a specific number of résumés, and do follow-up each week, and meet these goals. Realize your first interview—or your second—will not result in a job offer (unless you are unusually blessed), but that a thorough, effective job hunt campaign should result in several interviews, as well as valuable contacts which may last a lifetime.

- When you are rejected, try to get the most out of it, and don't take it too personally. Call and ask if you can obtain another interview; ask the reason for the rejection; ask for suggestions on how to improve your qualifications; or ask if the interviewer can recommend anyone who can use someone with your skills and background. Be cordial, grateful for any information you receive, and non-defensive. The results may surprise you.

- Learn to say no when confronted by a request you suspect will probably be stressful or time-consuming. It's just not possible to please everybody and be "superman" or "superwoman." If you are asked to write a sample business plan or PR proposal—and you know in your gut the job will not interest you, never mind waiting for the job offer—you are not compelled to meet this demand.

ADVICE FOR RECENT COLLEGE GRADUATES

It's difficult enough for an interviewer to predict if an applicant will work out well in the job in question, but it's particularly difficult if the job hunter is a recent college graduate—an untested quantity. Like other job-seekers, you need to demonstrate you have the experience, skills, and key personality traits that match the job. The only problem: your work history is so brief—namely, because your life has been so brief up to this point. You may have little to sell to the college recruiter, human resources professional, or employment agency except your enthusiasm, energy, and ability as a quick learner. The solution is to cull all your experience, both paid and nonpaid, which might possibly be relevant—summer and part-time jobs, volunteer work, tutoring, extracurricular activities, internships, sports, and hobbies.

Describe your experience in terms that demonstrate you learned important business and leadership skills. For example, not "I worked summers in my uncle's hardware store," but "took inventory, trained part-time employees, managed the store on Saturdays, designed new signage and ads." Instead of "I organized the senior prom," say "supervised a $3,000 budget, coordinated all arrangements with caterer and band, and designed flyers and ads, which led to a 15% increase in revenues over the year before." If you backpacked alone in Europe for three months one summer, funding your trip by working as a waitperson—making all your plane, train, and bus arrangements yourself—this shows initiative and independence. It's a shame to just say you "traveled in Europe" and let the interviewer think Mom and Dad footed the bill and did all the planning.

Grades are less important to many companies than you may think. If you have outstanding grades, class rankings, awards, and scholarships, excellent. However, employers often prefer a well-rounded person who has proven the ability to juggle several different things at once to one who has narrowly focused on school alone. Outside activities and team sports prove that you can work with others in a group toward a common goal and that you have other interests. If as president of the French club you arranged for speakers from the French consulate on culture, cuisine, and politics—a first for the club—say so. And you weren't just a counselor at Camp Hiawatha—you "instructed 30–40 young girls in nature study, planned and led hikes and games."

Be prepared to articulate reasons why you want to work in the industry, as well as at the company where you are interviewing. It may be an entry-level job at a low salary, but tremendous competition exists—particularly in "glamour" industries like entertainment, TV, journalism, public relations and advertising—so any edge you can demonstrate over your peers will help immensely. A starry-eyed "I've always loved watching movies" (or commercials, or reading books) won't do. Communicate your passion and interest by describing any early involvement in the field—writing short stories as a child, editing the school newspaper, booking club dates for local bands formed by your friends—and by doing your homework. Read newspaper, magazine, and trade articles about the industry and company, and talk to people in the field, just as if you were vying for a higher-level position. You needn't know every last thing about the company: just enough to gain a basic working knowledge and carry on an intelligent conversation.

One thing employers love to hear is that you helped support yourself during college through jobs and loans—which shows independence and a strong work ethic—instead of letting your parents foot the bill. So if you did, by all means speak up.

Internships can be particularly valuable in landing a job—they prove to an employer you have the experience, as well as the desire—regardless of whether they are paid or nonpaid. A tremendous variety exists, in terms of the work involved, eligibility by college students, graduates, and even career-changers, salary (some are quite generous), perquisites (some offer free meals, cars, round-trip travel, and even housing), and location. Opportunities range from the U.S. Senate, FBI, Marvel Comics, CIA, and National Basketball Association to top firms in entertainment, advertising, and aerospace. Some offer loads of busy-work—and close contact with the photocopy machine and coffee-maker—while others sizzle with exciting, productive tasks, plus the added bonus of meeting and mingling with leading figures in the field.

Companies look very kindly upon their interns. For example, in the near future, 70% of all college graduates hired by Intel, the world's foremost computer chip manufacturer, will be from its former interns. Consult various directories to locate internships which may be of interest to you.

Let's look at the top 10 "dream" internships in the country, according to *The Princeton Review Student Access Guide to America's Top 100 Internships*, which surveyed 1,600 former interns and investigated 2,000 paid and nonpaid programs.

ABBOT LABORATIES

This health care products company has a 12-week summer internship program, where about 150–200 interns work in areas from manufacturing to product development to research at its headquarters near Chicago. Salaries are $340–$1,000 per week, plus free housing, round-trip travel, and seminars.

APPLE COMPUTER

Interns work in computer development, marketing, design, and other areas in the company's 12-week summer internship program near San Francisco. In addition to setting their own hours, interns earn salaries of $600–$1,100 per week, plus seminars and sports events.

BOEING

All interns experience "test-flying" planes on this aircraft manufacturer's flight simulators during six-month as well as summer internships.

CORO FOUNDATION

Nine-month public service internships are available for 48 interns, who work in government agencies, community groups, labor unions, and so on in New York, Los Angeles, San Francisco, and St. Louis.

INTEL

About 800 interns work on design, engineering, and other areas in programs lasting from eight weeks to eight months for this computer chip manufacturer in the West and Southwest. Salaries are $450–$1,000 per week, plus rental cars, seminars, and round-trip travel.

LUCASFILM

While interns earn low salaries during 9-to-12 week internships, the lucky 15–20 who are chosen get the opportunity to work in TV or film production, model making, visual effects, and other areas at this company founded by *Star Wars* mastermind George Lucas.

MICROSOFT

The 350 summer interns hired by the computer software giant in Redmond, Washington, work in software testing, development, marketing, and other areas. Most salaries are about $9 per hour.

NATIONAL TROPICAL BOTANICAL GARDEN

On the island of Kauai, Hawaii, six interns work in the garden's collections, conservation, and other programs for 10–18 weeks—and explore other parts of Hawaii for work and recreation.

TBWA

At this New York advertising agency, 8–12 summer interns work in market research, account management, or media.

WASHINGTON POST

During a 12-week summer program, 15–20 interns report and write stories and enjoy weekly luncheons with editors or reporters. Salaries are $730 per week.

The authors of the internship book, Mark Oldman and Samer Hamadeh, who have served as interns everywhere from MTV, the U.S. Supreme Court, Capitol Records, and the Hoover Institution, offer the following tips on how to obtain internships:

- Fantasize. Think about careers which fire your passion.
- Scrap. Research the possibilities, consulting every source from college alumni, family connections, career centers, to the library.

- Don't procrastinate. Check deadlines. Some internship deadlines hit in November and April. Early applications increase your chances.
- Materialize. Assemble your application materials: résumé, cover letter, recommendations, transcripts, samples of your work.
- Customize. Write a special cover letter for each application, and tailor your résumé as well.
- Personalize. If possible, visit the internship sites for an interview, or make a personal call to the internship coordinator.
- Energize. Passion and persistence pay off. Follow up your letters, phone calls, and interviews with personal notes.
- Initiate. Create your own internship: write a letter asking a company that interests you for an internship, after researching the company.
- It's never too late. Many companies consider intern applications all year long. If you've missed a deadline, apply now for next year.

A sample job applicant evaluation form used by college recruiters for Coopers & Lybrand, a "Big Six" accounting firm, is included on the following two pages. Note how candidates are evaluated in detail in six areas (and how only two include academic record): client service capacity, full-service results, new business acquisition, staff development, technical/industry/functional specialization, and professional/community involvement. Pretty heady criteria for a recent college graduate, you may say. "Must hire" applicants should be "able to balance a demanding schedule including work, school, and outside activities," have a "wide variety of interests and experiences," and a "consistent record in coaching, tutoring, supervising others in work/social/campus activities."

Coopers & Lybrand | **Candidate Record**

NAME (LAST NAME FIRST)

COLLEGE NAME

□□□□□□□□□□□□□□□□□□□□□□□

Professional Requirements

NO HIRE	POSSIBLE HIRE	PROBABLE HIRE	MUST HIRE
	CLIENT SERVICE CAPACITY		

□	• Able to handle an acceptable schedule, including work, school and outside activities
	• Results-oriented
	• Aware of available resources and technology
	
	□
		• Able to handle moderate schedule, including work, school and outside activities
		• Achieves quality results as evidenced through:
		  • class standing
		  • scholarships
		  • awards
		  • promotions
		  • leadership roles
		• Makes reasonable use of available resources, including technology, to accomplish tasks
		• Meets deadlines
		□
			• Able to balance demanding schedule, including work, school and outside activities
			• Frequently/consistently achieves quality results as evidenced through:
			  • class standing
			  • scholarships
			  • awards
			  • promotions
			  • leadership roles
			• Solid record of using all available resources, including technology, to accomplish tasks
			• Evidences sense of urgency, responsiveness and ability to meet deadlines
			□

COMMENTS

_____
_____
_____

NO HIRE	POSSIBLE HIRE	PROBABLE HIRE	MUST HIRE
	FULL-SERVICE RESULTS		
□	• Has some outside interests and experiences • Asks routine questions □	• Has sufficient breadth in interests and experiences • Asks questions pertinent to the Firm, the profession, business • Knowledgeable about current business issues □	• Demonstrates a wide variety of interests and experiences • Asks penetrating questions that demonstrate an intellectual curiosity • Demonstrates a broad understanding of today's business issues • Resourceful in introducing and applying new approaches □

COMMENTS

_____
_____
_____

NO HIRE	POSSIBLE HIRE	PROBABLE HIRE	MUST HIRE
	NEW BUSINESS ACQUISITION		
□	• Demonstrates some knowledge of the profession, the Firm and business issues • Acceptable self-presentation □	• Sufficiently familiar with the Firm, the profession and business issues • Effective self-presentation (articulate, poised, confident, prepared) • Potential for influencing others □	• Actively pursues opportunities to gain meaningful knowledge of the Firm, profession and business issues • Outstanding self-presentation • Evidence of candidate's ability to influence others (classroom/work/campus or other activities) • Demonstrates strong desire to succeed in a competitive environment □

COMMENTS

_____
_____
_____

8/93

NO HIRE	POSSIBLE HIRE	PROBABLE HIRE	MUST HIRE

STAFF DEVELOPMENT

	POSSIBLE HIRE	PROBABLE HIRE	MUST HIRE
☐	• Shows interest in working with people • Positive contributor in a team environment ☐	• Has some experience in coaching, tutoring, supervising others • Demonstrates initiative in fostering teamwork ☐	• Has consistent record in coaching, tutoring, supervising others in work/social/campus activities • Demonstrates initiative in setting goals, building the team and achieving results • Sought out by others for advice and demonstrates a strong willingness to help ☐

COMMENTS _____
_____
_____

TECHNICAL, INDUSTRY, FUNCTIONAL SPECIALIZATION

	POSSIBLE HIRE	PROBABLE HIRE	MUST HIRE
☐	• Achieved acceptable level of academic record (consider major GPA, overall GPA and trends) ☐	• Achieved strong academic record (Consider major GPA, overall GPA and trends) • Seeks opportunities for technical growth and relevant business experience • Strong evidence of intellectual capacity ☐	• Achieved outstanding academic record with demanding course load and complexity • Solid record of achieving technical growth and relevant business experience through: • internships • assistance to faculty • professional organizations • research projects • Demonstrates outstanding intellectual capacity with judgement and common sense ☐

COMMENTS _____
_____
_____

PROFESSIONAL/COMMUNITY INVOLVEMENT

	POSSIBLE HIRE	PROBABLE HIRE	MUST HIRE
☐	• Involvement as a member in appropriate campus/professional/social activities ☐	• Active involvement in organizations through: • committees • projects • Supports others in achieving the organization's programs and goals ☐	• Attains leadership positions in meaningful professional/campus/social/classroom activities • Evidence of accomplishments that enhance and add value to the quality of the organization ☐

COMMENTS _____
_____
_____

CAMPUS INTERVIEW SUMMARY

OVERALL ASSESSMENT	INVITE	DATE AVAILABLE	AREA OF INTEREST	OFFICES PREFERRED
Must Hire ☐ Probable Hire ☐ Possible Hire ☐ No Hire ☐	☐ YES ☐ NO		☐ BA ☐ TAX ☐ PI ☐ HRAG ☐ ITAS ☐ FAS	No. 1 _____ No. 2 _____

If "Must Hire" please provide evidence on the following—broad thinker, strong work ethic, outstanding self-presentation and team player.

_____
_____
_____
_____
_____
_____

CHAPTER SIX

100 Interview Questions and Answers

PERSONAL/GENERAL

Q. *"Tell me about yourself." (Or "How would you describe yourself?")*

Often described as a "stress" question—which either paralyzes job-seekers into stunned silence or spurs an attack of the rambles—this is actually a splendid invitation to market yourself. You have the opportunity to showcase your qualifications for the job, and present a condensed history of your professional background. Present a unified pattern in broad brushstrokes which makes a strong case that you are ideal for the job in question—no more than two minutes, tops. The interviewer can always ask you to elaborate later on certain aspects of your career or education.

Some career experts even call this a "dream" question—but only if you're prepared. This is because it offers the opportunity to tell the most important things about yourself in an open-ended way in a manner of your own choosing. In your answer, start with where you are *now* in your career and give a summary of the qualifications that make you perfect for the job in question. For example: "I'm a marketing manager with eight years of experience in cosmetics and considerable success in repositioning products. For Velveteen liquid makeup, I led a team that created a new advertising campaign, redesigned the packaging, and targeted the Generation X market in particular, which resulted in a 30 percent increase in sales over the past year." Rehearse your two-minute pitch until it falls trippingly off your tongue and sounds convincing and spontaneous, not mechanical.

Q. "What are your greatest strengths?"

Pick a couple of the key personality traits employers desire from Chapter 5—drive, reliability, determination, or problem-solving skills, for example. But just saying "I'm very reliable," or "I have lots of drive," won't convince anyone. Give examples from your jobs to demonstrate that you indeed possess the traits you claim.

Q. "What is your greatest weakness?"

Don't place your foot in your mouth and turn confessional here—being painfully honest about your faults won't score you any points with the interviewer. A safe answer is to turn a positive trait into a "weakness." It's hard for an employer to look unkindly upon someone who is hardworking to the point of being a workaholic or a perfectionist, motivated to the point of being driven, or as demanding of team members as of himself or herself. Such weaknesses a company can live with, and even make a profit with in the process. Another safe answer: mention a former weakness you have overcome. For example, you now possess excellent time management skills since earlier in your career you failed to allot enough time to sales calls and writing up sales reports. Another option: state candidly your analytical skills are weaker than your people skills.

Q. "What are your most important accomplishments?"

These should spring to mind due to the writing exercises you performed to assemble your résumé in Chapter 2. Did you help your company make money, save money, save time, or become more efficient in any way? Explain how. Be aware that most job accomplishments are achieved as part of a team or department. Consequently, don't make it sound as though you single-handedly turned a situation around or executed a triumph by yourself—unless you truly did. Interviewers are quick to spot someone who takes credit for others' accomplishments.

Q. "Why did you pick that company (or college)?"

The interviewer is looking for sound reasoning and judgment behind some of your choices, as well as the ability to articulate it. Don't act as though you went wherever the wind blew. If the small company offered a great growth opportunity, or the large firm offered an excellent management training program and the chance to progress within the ranks, say so. If you went to a public college because this was all you could afford, say so.

Q. "Can you handle pressure?"

Of course, saying "yes" will not convince anyone. Explain how you turned out a professional work product despite juggling many competing projects, or despite a short deadline, or whatever the specific pressure was. It's also recommended to note that you generally plan and manage your time well to avoid panic deadlines.

Q. "How do you handle deadlines?"

Explain that you plan ahead for the materials and staff you need to handle a project, anticipate when certain steps need to be started and completed, and build in a time cushion to prevent last-minute panic.

Q. "Why should I hire you?"

This offers an excellent opportunity to trumpet your two-minute pitch showing why you are the ideal person for the job. Summarize your qualifications and your positive personality traits—matching each point of the interviewer's job description with what you offer. Cite an example or two of how you can make a contribution to the job, based on your past job performance.

Q. "Why didn't you go on to (or finish) college?"

Don't be defensive—realize an opportunity to show yourself as a hard-charger impatient to get started in the work world, or as someone who felt a lot could be learned by traveling around the world and sampling different cultures for a year, or joining the Peace Corps, etc. In other words, demonstrate quickly and confidently that what you did instead was valuable experience for the corporate world.

Q. "Are you willing to relocate?"

If you want the job, the answer is "yes." However, remember that you never have to make a decision about a job until an offer is made to you—and the job and/or the salary may be considerably reshaped by then.

Q. "Do you think your grades accurately reflect your ability?"

If you had high grades, the answer obviously is yes. If you didn't, say no, but describe other things which do demonstrate your ability—your part-time or full-time job during college, which taught you responsibility and specific skills, your leadership role in extracurricular activities, your internship at a local radio or TV station, taking care of or financially supporting a sick parent, volunteer work at a local hospital once a week, etc. Do this without being defensive—grades matter very little to an employer after that first post-college job, since all he or she really wants is a good employee who will perform the job well and be manageable.

Q. "What motivates you to put forth your greatest effort?"

Disabuse the interviewer of the suspicion that a generous salary, gigantic title, and corner office are your prime motivators. Explain that, to you, a job well-done is its own best reward since your own work and ethic demand it, but that kind words of appreciation from your boss are always welcome. Add that you, like everyone, look forward to regular salary reviews.

Q. "What have you done that shows initiative?"

Think of something which demonstrates a take-charge attitude where you came up with an idea and acted on it for the greater good of your company. The action you took should not have flouted corporate rules and procedures. Perhaps you drew up a flowchart for everyone in your division that organized multiple tasks and deadlines for a major conference or grand opening you were working on.

If you are a recent college graduate, you can cite the time you started a typing service for your fellow students' term papers and employed three students part-time—or the time you traveled to Europe for two months alone, made all your own travel arrangements, and funded it through part-time jobs.

Q. "If you could live your life over again, what would you do differently?"

The interviewer is looking less for the "right" answer than for how you think, how you assess yourself, and what makes you tick to see if you are a good fit for the company. Show maturity, perspective, and sound reasoning in your answer, and mention only one thing or nothing. Perhaps you would have traveled the globe more, experienced different cultures, and met many different types of people. Or perhaps you are content, look forward to every day with enthusiasm and vigor, have no regrets, and would have changed nothing.

Q. "What did you learn in your college career?"

The interviewer is not as interested in the subject matter you learned as in if you developed some key personality traits necessary in the work world, such as disciplined work habits, reliability, initiative, etc. (He or she is hoping for proof you did not spend all your time partying and living off your parents' money.)

Q. "Describe your ideal job."

Describe a job which matches the description of the job given you by the interviewer, which enables you to use your qualifications and skills to grow and make a contribution to the company.

Q. "What was the last book (or movie) you read (or saw)? What did you think of it?"

Be sure you mention a book you have read or movie you have seen, not just the "hot" item of the moment, in case you are asked questions about it. Pick one that stimulated your thinking and taught you something useful in the work world—in other words, not the latest action thriller or horror flick.

Q. "Do you have any questions?"

The wrong answer is "no," or an extended "ummm." This generally means the interview is at an end, and so is your final opportunity to score some points. Demonstrate interest, enthusiasm, and knowledge about the company and its product or service one last time. If you can, ask at least one insightful question pegged to something you read in the business press or a trade magazine—why the company is succeeding with a new strategy, or more details about expansion in the division where you are interviewing. You'll look savvy and you'll encourage the interviewer to talk about a subject he or she is expert on—which often means you'll be regarded as an excellent conversationalist. Questions about salary, benefits, or vacation are out of line here. Wait for the job offer—without which you have no negotiating chip.

Q. "Which parent do you most resemble—your mother or your father—and why?"

Again, the interviewer is seeking not the "right" answer but what makes you tick, how you assess yourself and articulate reasons to back up your points. Pick personality traits helpful in the work world, and describe how you learned these from your parent.

Q. "Describe your educational background."

Starting with your most advanced degree first, mention the degrees and majors, omitting the schools—unless the school is particularly prestigious or unless the interviewer is a fellow alumnus or alumna. If you are not a college graduate, explain confidently and calmly that you entered the work world early, either by necessity or choice.

Q. "Do you have plans to continue your education?"

If you do, make clear that it will be done nights or weekends, so it will not interfere with your job.

Q. "How was your college education funded?"

Explain the proportion covered by a scholarship, part-time jobs, and loans. If you were responsible for 100% of your education, point it out—it never fails to impress.

Q. "What are your hobbies?"

This sounds like a harmless question, but usually the interviewer is trying to sound out if you will be a good fit for the corporate culture. Solitary pursuits such as reading, running, and biking indicate you prefer to be alone; sports such as baseball, softball, basketball, etc. indicate you feel comfortable being part of a team.

Q. "Can you take direction?"

Yes, you can, and you also welcome constructive criticism without feeling attacked because you understand you have a lot to learn from more experienced people in the company.

Q. "What are the reasons for your success?"

Offer general reasons, back them up with an example or two from your jobs, and mention the help from colleagues or managers—teamwork again—to avoid coming across like an egomaniac. Perhaps you have a great deal of drive, welcome mastering new skills, have indefatigable energy—you never leave the office before making one more phone call or writing one more letter, and have been lucky enough to have worked with exceptionally talented managers and staff.

Q. "What are some of your pet peeves?"

Name some things which bother any hard-working, employee— colleagues who do their work incompetently, are clock-watchers, are often absent forcing others to do their work, and complain about their lack of promotions or raises. Don't indicate in any way that such pecca-dilloes cause you to lose your temper, however—no one wants to hire a Vesuvius who is about to blow at any moment.

Q. "Are you a risk-taker?"

The interviewer wants to know if you take prudent risks backed by knowledge, good judgment and consultation with your boss—or if you are the type who flies off the handle and is apt to make a fool out of yourself and the company. Before you answer, ask what sort of risk the interviewer has in mind. This way, you have a better idea of how to frame your answer to describe how you evaluate a risk.

Q. "Which of your skills can stand improvement at this time?"

A clever way to cajole you into admitting your weaknesses. Say, instead, that from the interviewer's description you seem to have all the necessary skills and qualifications for the job, but that since one or two areas are so crucial, you believe in constantly updating and polishing your skills to do the best possible job. You're trying to make a diamond shine brighter, not confess to being only a rhinestone, in other words.

Q. "What was the hardest decision you ever had to make, and how did you handle it?"

A major work-related decision, such as firing staffers or radically re-shaping strategy to help an ailing division (which, of course, succeeded), your rationale, and how you carried it out is needed here. No need to confess your agonizing choice to put an aging parent in a nursing home, put your teenage son in a drug rehab program, or get a divorce. These may have been your most difficult decisions, but avoid the trap some job-seekers fall into when faced with a cordial, you-can-tell-me tone from an interviewer.

Q. "Who (or what) has been a major influence on your life?"

Who or what is less important than a sound rationale backing up why this made you into what you are today—a holder of key personality traits, such as integrity, determination, initiative, that are valuable to employers. Think carefully about your formative influences—parent, teacher, coach, minister—and offer a self-assessment which is on target.

Q. "What do you worry about?"

Don't open a window into your psyche and reveal what you truly worry about at 3:00 A.M.—what you'll do when the unemployment check runs out, family problems, crime, Presidential policies. Stick to things that are job-related and expected of a hard-working employee—what the competition is doing, deadlines, team members who are not pulling their weight, winning that new piece of business you've been eyeing—but note you aim to solve the situation, not just stew about it.

Q. "Why do you want to switch from the public to the private sector?"

While you have learned a great deal working for the government—specify what—you welcome the opportunity to work in an atmosphere where attention is paid to the bottom line, and where individual effort and decision-making is both expected and rewarded.

Q. "Are you a self-starter?"

If you say "yes" and stop dead, you aren't. Use this question as an opportunity to sell yourself and your proactive approach to your jobs. You know what to do and you go ahead and do it, without relying on constant direction and feedback from your manager. Offer the same examples as for "What have you done that shows initiative?"

Q. "How have you benefited from your disappointments?"

No need to cite specific disappointments which saddened or demoralized you, unless you are asked—just give a general idea of how you are a better person as a result. You analyzed these events to uncover the kernel which caused them, you know now how you would act differently at various points if the same situation arose, and you remember the lessons learned so they can be applied to new situations. As the philosopher George Santayana once said, "Those who cannot remember the past are condemned to fulfil it."

Q. "Can you think of a challenge you faced and how you dealt with it?"

Show how you aggressively launched a campaign or implemented strategy. For example, discuss the time your company, a video-game maker, was losing market share to a competitor that successfully wooed the preteen market with a very clever ad and public relations campaign. You declared all-out marketing warfare, and planned and carried out tactics—such as commissioning novels that were written about the video game, sending free T-shirts emblazoned with major characters if kids returned a coupon inside the box, a snazzy new ad campaign with an "800" number where callers could "talk" interactively with major characters, etc.—which succeeded in recapturing customers.

Q. "How do you plan your time?"

Show an organized, prioritized approach—the interviewer dislikes visions of people who hopscotch in an unfocused manner from one task to another, often missing out on major priorities. For example, perhaps you only return phone calls from midafternoon on, saving the rest of the day for client meetings, staff contact, thinking, and writing. You read correspondence and trade magazines after 5:00 P.M., and never leave before writing a "do list" for tomorrow. This way, you're ready to hit the ground running each morning.

Q. "Can we check your references?"

If you want a job offer, the answer is yes. But protect yourself—say you will be happy to provide references from current and former employers at the time a job offer is extended. Add that you want these references to be checked *after* you have accepted a written job offer and resigned from your current company. You want to avoid the horror of having your current employer, who is not even aware you are job-hunting, being called for a reference, then failing to receive a job offer—and perhaps being terminated by your irate employer. (It happens.)

Q. "How do you handle rejection?"

For jobs in sales, public relations, and similar fields, rejection is a part of life. Answer that you do not take it personally and let it get you down; you forge ahead and make more phone calls or customer sales calls, since you realize the field is a numbers game with a high ratio of failures to successes.

Q. "Are you happy with your life?"

The answer is "yes." If you aren't, keep it to yourself or share it with family, friends, or your therapist. Employers don't want you to stew about personal problems or anxieties on their time—and lose productivity in the process.

WORK HISTORY

Q. "What don't you like about your current (previous) employer?"

You like everything about your current or previous employer. Don't let words like personality conflict, outmoded business practices, unfair promotion systems, and other forms of criticism escape your lips. Interviewers assume, rightly or wrongly, that if you badmouth one employer, you will badmouth the next. A company does not willingly hire someone who is a potential troublemaker. Reserve job horror stories for friends and relatives. At your interview, say you learned a tremendous amount from your last employer and the experience was indispensable for your career. You highly respect the professionalism and judgment of your boss, and so on.

Q. "How long have you been looking for a job?"

Not to worry if you already hold a job. Your answer: You are now seeking a job that will challenge you at this stage of your career and a company that will provide opportunities for career growth.

If, however, you are unemployed, be very careful how you answer. A flat "year and a half" or "two years" will not exactly draw job offers in droves. If you have been doing constructive activities in the meantime—such as helping out in your son's business, learning a new skill, studying for your broker's license, consulting, or chairing the fund-raising committee of your favorite charity—by all means say so. Subtract this time from the time you have been unemployed, so that the time you have been actively looking for a job full-time is much shorter.

Avoid sounding defensive or chastened if you are unemployed. Interviewers want people who are "hot commodities," so act like the desirable candidate you are. Note that you have weighed other job offers in the meantime, but that you are being particular about the job and environment you choose so you can be challenged. Remember, *how* you answer an interview question is often as important as the content of what you say.

Q. "What do you know about our company?"

Sound informed about the company's products or services, growth areas, future plans, etc.—in other words, the sort of information you learned when you researched the company, as discussed in Chapter 1. Positives only, please—don't remind the interviewer of the failure of the introduction of Product X or how much stock prices have fallen since the recent government investigation. You have no business being in a job interview if you have not prepared yourself to discuss the company and its prospects.

Q. "Which jobs (or duties) have you enjoyed most?"

Your answer should be jobs or duties which enabled you to showcase some of the key personality traits employers desire and which, ideally, resemble the job you are presently interviewing for.

Q. "Which jobs (or duties) have you enjoyed least?"

It doesn't speak well for you to admit to holding jobs that were dead-end or stultifyingly dull. The interviewer will wonder why you stayed. Try to find something the job taught you, or how it helped you develop one of the key personality traits employers desire.

Q. "I understand you're working for a really tough firm (sweatshop, pressure-cooker, etc.) now. What's it like?"

Sometimes interviewers try to cajole you into making critical remarks about your current (or former) employer. Don't. Capitalize on the positive aspects of what you learned and how you can transfer that knowledge to the job in question. "Play dumb" about any negative labels the interviewer uses—he or she will only respect your discretion and unwillingness to fall for this ploy.

Q. "Can you sell me on our product (or service or concept)?"

It's not as difficult as it sounds to do a sales presentation for a company's product or services. You should already be prepared because of the research you did before the interview. Calmly and confidently, act as if you are on a sales call: enumerate the major selling features, note if the product or service is unique in any way, and how it differs from its competition. The interviewer is looking for sales ability, good communication skills, and the ability to think quickly under pressure.

Q. "Why did you leave your last job (or want to leave your current job)?"

Cite one of the few acceptable reasons: you wanted greater responsibility, more challenge, higher salary, larger company for specialization (or smaller company for opportunity), or more job security. If you are a career-changer, explain that you enjoyed your previous career, but have always wanted to work in this field and finally decided to go for it.

Q. "Which trade journals do you read?"

The answer to this question should never be "What is a trade journal?" Even if you are applying for an entry-level the position, you should be familiar with the trade journals in your industry, and be aware of the differences between them.

Q. "What are some mistakes you've made in your previous jobs?"

Uh-oh—you're being invited to tell tales against yourself. Whatever you admit to, make sure it's fairly innocuous and didn't involve losing money or time for your company. Be quick to explain what you learned from a past mistake and how you rectified things. For example, perhaps you didn't document your activities or keep your boss up to date as much as you should have, making it difficult for others to fill in when you were out sick or on vacation. But once you were admonished as to how this inconveniences your co-workers, you now keep one of the most thorough paper trails in your firm.

Q. "What have you learned from your mistakes in your jobs?"

You should have stated what you learned in your answer to the previous question, to deflect this one. Show that you benefit from constructive criticism and do not take it personally, and that you have acquired one of the key personality traits employers desire (team player, initiative, determination, etc.).

Q. "Where else are you applying for a job?"

It's okay to admit to interviewing at other firms, but don't say where. If pressed, politely decline to say. While it's all right to convey the idea you are wanted, it's a bad idea to get into a sparring match dropping names of other firms, positions, and salary. Don't communicate the impression that this job is a fall-back or that your first choice lies elsewhere. Above all, if you are seeking a different type of job elsewhere—or in a different industry altogether—do not admit it. You may be covering all your bases in a tough economy, but it will only alarm the interviewer to know you are considering jobs in widely divergent fields.

Q. "Why have you changed jobs several times in the past few years?"

A charge of job-hopping is much less serious today than it used to be, since the days of lifetime employment are over. However, emphasize that you learned something in every job, which you can now bring to your new company. This may take some persuasion, but convince the interviewer you have been moving steadily toward more professional growth and greater responsibility, and that you firmly believe the position you are interviewing for offers the challenges you require. Point out that you have also developed flexibility in adapting to different work environments—a real plus in today's world, and a trait that someone mired in the same company for a decade or more may not possess.

Q. "Since you've job-hopped a lot in the past few years, isn't it possible you will be bored working here?"

No—because this job offers you the challenges you've been seeking your entire life. Elaborate a bit on why these challenges intrigue you and how you plan to handle them, to deflect attention from your job-hopping past and direct it toward your soon-to-be settled and stable present with this company.

Q. "Why were you fired?"

Of course, this question comes not because you volunteered this information, but because the interviewer is aware you have been fired. If your job was one of hundreds of thousands eliminated through downsizing—a very common occurrence today—point this out, as it removes most of the onus from you. If your former company has high turnover figures, either resignations or firings, cite these figures, since this shows your leaving was not an isolated incident. If you were fired for cause, present the facts in the most positive light possible and state that the problem has been rectified. Perhaps a former boss, or former client, is willing to say good words about your performance. State who will be happy to give references. Whatever you do, don't badmouth your employer for firing you, and don't act defensive and discouraged—this will make it tougher, not easier, to find another position.

Q. "Are you willing to take a drug test as a condition of employment?"

The only answer is "yes" if you are at all interested in getting a job offer. Drug testing has become very common today as employers try to screen out prospective employees who are drug abusers.

Before a test is actually administered, a company should give you a form to sign authorizing your permission, which should name all the prescription and over-the-counter drugs and foods believed to cross-react with the test. List all the drugs and medications you have taken in recent weeks, as well as the foods named on the form.

It may surprise you to learn that many substances, such as cold medications, ibuprofen, tranquilizers, and even poppy-seed bagels, can cause positive results on drug tests and thus unfairly brand you as a drug user. If you are not offered a form to sign that lists these substances, say politely that while you are willing to be tested, you would like to know which substances can cross-react with the test because you are familiar with articles on this subject. If the firm does not give you a list, weigh the risk of the test and your interest in a job offer—perhaps you can suggest that your family doctor conduct the test.

Q. "How do you feel about working overtime?"

You understand there are times when a company expects employees to pitch in with extra effort and extra hours, and this is fine with you. The interviewer wants to find out if you are a 9-to-5 clock-watcher, so cite an example from a past job where you expended extra hours to get a project completed.

Q. "Describe a difficult situation at work and how you handled it."

While the interviewer wants to probe your problem-solving skills, you have the chance to demonstrate some of the key personality traits employers desire as well, such as listening skills, initiative, determination, etc. For example: As a supervisor with a difficult client, I listened to the demands of the client and my staff, suggested compromises where needed, and implemented new suggestions.

Q. "You've probably heard some bad things about our company. What are they and how do you feel about them?"

No, you haven't. You know the company is a leader in its field and expects employees to work hard and produce. This is exactly what you are looking for, and you are eager to make a contribution.

Q. "How many hours a week do you work?"

Since workaholism is a virtue, not a vice, in today's lean and mean companies, the more hours you can cite, the better. However, say that you also try to plan and manage your time so you are as productive as possible, just in case the company believes long hours denote poor time management and an inability to delegate.

Q. "How would you do this job differently from other people?"

Demonstrate that your mix of skills and key personality traits is a winning combination which will do a bang-up job. If you are not aware of all the challenges the job presents, ask; then, explain a creative approach to handling at least one of them.

Q. "Have you done your best work yet?"

Say "yes" and kiss a job offer good-bye—no one wants to hire someone who has already peaked. You've performed well, in your opinion, but believe there is still lots you can contribute.

Q. "How do you rate your career progress to date?"

Show a healthy sense of self-respect and note that while you are proud of your accomplishments and have learned a great deal about the industry within the specific sphere of your jobs, the best is yet to come.

Q. "What aspects of your job do you rate as most important?"

Prioritize which of your duties most impact your company's bottom line, i.e., which make money, save time, or increase efficiency. Show that you are not missing the forest for the trees and are not wasting precious time and effort on inessentials.

Q. "What personality traits do you think are necessary to succeed in this field?"

Cite some of the key personality traits we have discussed all along, highlighting those which may be especially important in your chosen field, based on your own research or hints from the interviewer.

Q. "Describe your current job responsibilities."

List your duties, but with an eye to how they fit into the mission of the company as a whole. An employer does not want someone with tunnel vision, who sees his or her job as the be-all and end-all, but a person with a sense of interrelatedness who functions as part of a team.

Q. "What do you like the most about this job?"

Answer this only after you have ascertained the main problem the interviewer wants solved in this job. If you are uncertain, ask to clarify the projects which need immediate attention, the overall mission of the division at present, etc. Then say you are eager to tackle this challenge, and explain why you are well suited in terms of qualifications and key personality traits to do so.

Q. "Who do you see as our company's competition, and why?"

You have learned the answer to this question from your preinterview research on the company, which included reading the business press and trade magazines. Name a few firms that offer similar products or services, and what differentiates them from this company—price, quality, availability, marketing strategy, etc.

Q. "How is our company superior to others in its field?"

From your research, you should be able to cite a few areas where this company shines.

Q. "How do you keep abreast of new developments in your field?"

You regularly read trade magazines and the business press, and attend trade association meetings and an occasional seminar or conference. Perhaps you have also used your company's tuition reimbursement program to take classes to brush up on skills or learn new ones.

Q. "Since you are a career-changer, why do you think you can do this job?"

Face it: if you've done sales in one field, you can do it in another; if you've worked with medical clients at a public relations and advertising agency, you can be director of PR and advertising at a hospital; if you've written in-house newsletters in one industry, this skill can benefit another. Convince the interviewer you have the skills the job requires, and that they can easily be transferred to a new environment.

You can also add that, in addition to the skills other applicants for this job possess, you bring something extra and valuable to the table—perhaps a solid knowledge of the teenage market or financial knowledge. Even if there seems to be no obvious connection between your former career and the job, uncover some similar skill or aspect of your work history or education which is relevant.

Q. "You are reentering the labor market after an absence of 15 years. Why do you think you can do the job?"

Emphasize how your skills and accomplishments in volunteer work for charities, schools, churches, or synagogues, nonpaid work experience in helping out relatives' businesses, managing and budgeting your household's finances, and hobbies are transferable to the job. Also explain which key personality traits you will bring to the job.

Q. "How soon can you start?"

Two weeks' notice is generally expected as the minimum in giving notice to your current employer and making sure your workload is covered. In cases where you have been at the firm for many years, you may want to give more notice.

Q. "What do you like least about this job?"

Pick something very minor and unconnected to the main goals dear to any company's heart—making money, saving money, or saving time. Doing those expense reports, updating press lists, taking calls from vendors pitching their services—all are acceptable.

Q. "I'm not sure you have the right qualifications (or are suitable) for this position."

Not to worry—it's not as bad as it sounds. The interviewer may simply be saying "sell me." Even if the interviewer isn't, act innocently as though he or she is. Don't react as if this is a kiss-off, with shock or discomfiture, and don't be argumentative. Inquire calmly if he or she is concerned about any particular area. Then, mildly but firmly reassure the interviewer of the strength of your skills in this area—give an example or two—or, concede that while this area is not your strong point, similar skills, extensive experience, and personality traits you possess more than compensate for the lack. You have always been a quick study, unafraid of new challenges, and your rapid promotions in your previous jobs demonstrate this, for example. If you are a career-changer or have performed a similar job in a different setting, empha-size the transferability of these skills. The interviewer, you see, is look-ing not only for a substantive answer but for confidence and grace under pressure, as well as your astuteness in hearing the true message behind this statement. Don't disappoint.

Q. "Wouldn't you feel more comfortable at another firm?"

Don't be paranoid and assume you're being shown the door or getting a hint you'd be better off with "your kind of people" elsewhere. Be calm, confident, and undeterred, and regard this as another "sell me" question. Ask the interviewer what he or she means and counter any objections with why your qualifications and key personality traits are a good match for the job. Demonstrate your knowledge about this firm and name specific contributions you can make right away.

FUTURE GOALS

Q. "Where do you expect to be in five (three) years?"

A foolish question in today's fast-paced, downsized world, but sometimes still asked. You doubtless don't know where you will be in five years—and the interviewer probably doesn't know where he or she will be, either. However, to be on the safe side, say you expect to be with the same company in the area where your skills and talents can serve the firm the most, in a position of greater responsibility. If you can identify the area which is the fastest-growing—from your research or from what the interviewer has told you—say so.

It's also all right to say that while you can not predict specifics, you hope to take advantage of opportunities and growth areas as they arise, and let your skills and talents take you as far as they can. It's best not to name a specific job title, but to concentrate on the work itself. Promotability in a firm depends on some factors beyond your control, such as a willing boss or employees with more seniority than you. Above all, don't be like the woman who, unenthused about the job she was applying for—her first love was the music industry—spontaneously replied, "Not here."

Q. "Since you were in the same job for such a long time, you've probably grown very comfortable in it—maybe a bit stale. How would you cope with a new job in a company such as ours?"

You welcome new challenges and the opportunity for more professional growth, which is why you are ready to move on. You've learned a great deal and hope to make a contribution based upon what you've learned. You are eager to learn new things and would like to hear more about the challenges you would face in this job.

Q. "What are you looking for in your next job?"

Couch what you seek in terms of what you can offer the employer, not what the employer can offer you, such as glamour, travel, etc. For example, "I am seeking a company where I can apply my proven ability to tap underutilized markets and motivate sales staff, and grow as much as I can professionally. When I was at ABC Company, I . . . ."

Q. "How long would you stay with our company?"

The best answer is that you are very interested in the company and intend to stay as long as you are facing challenges and growing as a professional. If you have a stable work history marked by long periods at various companies, point this out. If not, emphasize that this is the company you want to settle down with. Ask about which specific projects you can get involved with immediately.

Q. "What is your next career step?"

Your next step matches the description of the job the interviewer has given you perfectly, and you are eager to make a contribution based on your proven ability in (sales, supervision, quality control, copywriting, etc.). Show how this next step will benefit the company (and you only incidentally).

Q. "Why do you want to change careers at this point in your life?"

While you have enjoyed your former career, you have always had an innate talent and hankering for this field, regularly read its trade magazines as a hobby, and are ready and eager to make a change and "go for it."

Q. "When do you expect to be promoted?"

The wrong answer is to name a specific time—like six months, a year, or three years—which brands you as cocky and arrogant. To be safe, answer that you expect to grow steadily in skills and experience so you will be ready when an opportunity is ripe in the company, and you are sure your performance will merit a promotion over time since you always try to do the best possible job you can.

Q. "Why do you want to get into this field (or get this job)?"

It never fails to astonish and irritate interviewers when candidates cannot respond. Your answer should display some insight about how the industry works or what the job really entails day to day. It should convey that you have thought about what you want. There are no "best" answers for different jobs, but you should beware of tired, meaningless clichés like "I just love people," or "I love to travel." Interviewers want to separate dreamers from doers.

Q. "What are your career goals and how do you plan to achieve them?"

You want to go as far as your skills and talents will take you, want to serve the company in the areas where you can be most useful, and meet all the challenges that arise so you can become the professional you aspire to be. Avoid annoying statements like "I want to be president of the firm someday," or "I really want your job": they don't convey ambition and drive, but arrogance and egocentricity.

TEAMWORK/LEADERSHIP

Q. "Have you ever had problems in dealing with other people?"

Your answer is no, you have always tried to be a team player and cooperate with others for the good of the company.

Q. "What kinds of people do you prefer to work with?"

People who are hard-working, honest, enthusiastic, and take pride in their work—in other words, people who share some of the key personality traits employers desire.

Q. "What kinds of people do you find it difficult to work with?"

People who possess the opposite of these traits—who lack a work ethic, are dishonest, are malcontents who complain incessantly, who don't pull together in a team effort.

Q. "Can you tell me about your management style?"

Your answer should involve the following: you motivate your staff by praise, rewards, and setting a good example; you treat them with respect, inviting their suggestions; you empower them to take on tasks of greater responsibility, and make them feel part of a team where everyone is pulling together; and you explain the long-term as well as the short-term goals of the work being done.

Q. "How do you feel about working for a woman executive?"

To you, a boss is a boss; any negative feelings on the subject should be kept to yourself.

Q. "Do you prefer working with others or alone?"

Before you answer, be sure you know what type of person the company is seeking for the job in question, either from your own research or from asking the interviewer. Be aware, however, that the vast majority of firms operate in a team environment, and that interpersonal skills are considered important even for most technical, writing, and other positions. If you truly want to work alone, consider self-employment—even then, You will deal with clients, suppliers, and so on. A safe answer: You prefer to work as part of a team, but can work alone if necessary since you don't require constant feedback and direction.

Q. "Can you take direction?"

Yes, you can, and you also welcome constructive criticism without feeling attacked because you understand you have a lot to learn from more experienced people in the company.

Q. "How do you operate as a team player?"

You realize that everyone on the team has an important and interdependent role to play, you listen to their opinions with respect, you try to get along with everyone for the greater good of the company, and you do your job in a manner that helps the team operate smoothly and productively.

Q. **"How do you get along with your current (or former) boss?"**

You get along fine with your current or former boss, and you respect his or her ability, judgment, and professionalism. Take the high road on this. Your boss may be an ogre who rules with an iron hand, but intimations of this should never pass your lips.

Q. **"How do you deal with people with different backgrounds and value systems from your own?"**

You try to cooperate and get along with everyone to achieve the goals of the department and company as a whole. You enjoy working with different types of people as you learn new things and believe "variety is the spice of life."

SALARY

Q. **"Why aren't you making more money at your age?"**

Avoid being defensive. Smile, and say you have been building a career, honing your skills, learning a tremendous amount, and that money has not been your sole object. Now, however, you believe you offer a package of skills that is really worthwhile to an employer.

Q. **"What salary are you looking for (or what is your salary requirement)?"**

Try to buy time, and throw the question back into the interviewer's court. It's foolish to name a figure, and either cause the interviewer to chuckle inwardly at the absurdly cheap hire you are, or throw yourself out of the ring by asking for too much money. This is a game where whoever names a figure first, loses. First, list all the duties of the job according to the description you have been given to make sure you and the interviewer are on the same wavelength.

Then, ask what salary range he or she is allowed to offer for the job, or what salary range your skills and background are worth. Hopefully, you will hear a range straight from the interviewer's lips, from which you can negotiate. If all else fails—his or her lips are sealed—counter with a range, not a fixed figure, you are comfortable with.

Q. "That's a little high for us. Can you come down a little?"

All is not lost—throw the ball back. Ask the interviewer what he or she envisions as the salarly range, and negotiate with that range in mind. You instantly weaken your negotiating position if you cave in after five seconds and lower your figure.

Q. "How much money are you worth?"

Similar to asking the salary you want, this also demands you offer proof to back it up. Demonstrate an awareness of the market rate for the job based upon your skills and experience, and a confidence that your qualifications match the job requirements point by point when you name a range you are comfortable with.

Q. "What salary are you making now?"

Since employers display a distressing propensity to take your current salary into consideration when making a salary offer—generally offering about 10–15 percent more, if you are making market rates—answer this question with a great deal of care. Throw the ball back in the interviewer's court if you can, when you are making a below-market or above-market salary. If you are below market, try to get away with citing the market range for the job to provoke the interviewer into naming a figure. If you are making above market, also avoid naming a figure; instead express interest in the job and confidence in reaching agreement. You should probably only baldly mention your current salary if you are making the market rate.

Q. "What salary do you expect to earn five years (or three years, etc.) from now?"

Of course, you don't even know what position you'll be holding at that point—or if you'll still be at the company. Ask the interviewer what would be a reasonable salary to expect for someone with your skills and background. If pressed, cite a range, based upon market rates, and a career path to back it up. It's best to be vague—"at that point I'll have six years of experience as an account supervisor in the pharmaceutical area" and avoid job titles.

Q. "You've been stuck in the same position at basically the same salary for the past five years at your current (or former) employer. Why?"

Ouch. If you've inadvertently disclosed this, you must deal with it. Explain that opportunities for advancement were very limited at your company, and that other employees with more seniority were ahead of you. If the last promotion in your division was a long time ago, cite the date. Add quickly that you are eager to assume more responsibility and have the skills and talent to do so—which is why you are interviewing at this firm today.

CHAPTER 7

Illegal Questions and Discrimination

When a California jury awarded $7.1 million to a female secretary who was sexually harassed by a partner at a major law firm in 1994, it sent a message that was hard for American employers to ignore: Courts will not sanction discrimination in the workplace.

Indeed, America's rapidly changing employment laws protect you more than ever before against illegal discrimination during job interviews. Protective federal laws include Title VII of the Civil Rights Act of 1964, the Age Discrimination in Employment Act (1967), the Pregnancy Discrimination Act (1978), and the Americans with Disabilities Act (1990). A potential employer may not prejudge you because of:

- sex
- age
- religion
- national origin
- physical disability
- pregnancy
- relationship with disabled individuals
- physical illness
- mental illness
- recovering alcoholism or drug addiction

QUESTIONS THAT INDICATE DISCRIMINATION

For a job applicant such as yourself, what does this all boil down to? Just this: interviewers may not ask certain questions that are considered prejudicial under the law. Interviewers should only ask questions that relate to skills required to do the job for which you are applying.

If an unwary interviewer poses any of the questions listed below, and you are later turned down for the position, you may be able to prevail in a discrimination lawsuit against the company.

SEXUAL DISCRIMINATION

Questions about marital status are illegal. And the following questions would likely *not* be posed to men. Therefore, in one way or another, they are evidence of bias:

"Are you married?"

"Will you be leaving the firm to raise children when you get married?"

"How will you take care of your children if you come to work here?"

"Will you be moving out of the region when your husband gets his Ph.D.?" This question was asked of a female job applicant in Arizona. The employer thought he was being nice, engaging in informal conversation.

"Are you expecting a child?" Pregnant applicants cannot be discriminated against.

Finally, if you are a man, watch out for a question like this:

"Would you have any difficulty working with our all-woman staff?" This question, if asked of a male applicant, could lead to a lawsuit for sex discrimination if the man is denied employment.

DISABILITY DISCRIMINATION

"Do you have a disability?"

"Have you ever filed for workman's compensation insurance?" Employers are not allowed to discriminate against individuals who have done so.

"Have you ever been addicted to drugs?" Recovering addicts and alcoholics are protected by law.

"Is any member of your family disabled?" Or, "How will you care for your disabled parent if you work here?" In the past, there were a lot of problems with employers discriminating against parents, spouses, or children of the disabled. Applicants were often denied employment because the businesses thought they would miss a lot of work or be unable to travel, in order to care for their relatives. The law explicitly prohibits employers from discriminating against these people.

Suppose you have a disability, and the employer asks you to demonstrate how you would perform a certain task required by the available position. Is this discrimination? It may not be if the request relates to job duties required by the position.

RACIAL DISCRIMINATION

"Would working with people of another race be a problem?"

"Would working for a manager of another race or religion be a problem?" A minority applicant who was asked this question and was later denied employment, charged that the question must have been racially motivated, and sued the employer.

The interviewer may not ask if you have a certain skill, unless that skill is required to carry out the duties of the available position. If it is not, the question may reveal bias, particularly if the skill is one few minority candidates are likely to have.

"Do you have a high school diploma/college degree?" That question is fine if, in fact, such a diploma or degree is necessary to carrying out the duties of the position for which you are applying. But it is dangerous if such education is not a requirement. One employer who asked this question was found to be discriminating against minority groups, which typically have a smaller percentage of individuals with high school diplomas.

OTHER BIAS

Here are some questions that may reflect bias against certain religions or national origins:

"Do you go to synagogue?"

"Are you active in your church?"

"Do you belong to any social clubs?"

"What country did your parents come from?"

These questions suggest bias against older workers:

"How many years has it been since you graduated from college?"

"Would you have any difficulty working for a boss who is younger than you?"

One final remark: It doesn't help matters if your interviewer tries to make a joke out of what would otherwise be an offensive remark. Biased remarks are just as damaging if made in fun—and just as damaging in a court of law.

So far we've covered questions that you may hear during the hiring interview. But there's something else to consider: written employment applications can also reveal bias. Application forms may reveal bias if they ask for:

- Race, color, sex, marital status, religion, age, national origin, or citizenship.
- Date of high school graduation. This may indicate age bias.
- Height or weight. This has led to discrimination against women and some nationalities.
- Foreign addresses. This may reflect bias against certain nationalities.

LAW AND THE INTERVIEW

While federal discrimination laws typically apply to employers with at least a dozen employees, state laws usually have smaller thresholds. California law against disability discrimination, for example, triggers at five workers and Connecticut law at three. To find out about your state laws, consult with your attorney or contact your local bar association.

Employers who have only a few workers are still subject to "common law" claims. ("Common law" refers to legal decisions that are based upon a history of previous jury decisions, not on actual statutes passed by state or federal legislative bodies.) In some cases such employers have been sued for intentional infliction of emotional distress, which can actually jack up the damages. All of this legal risk has put quite a damper on the job interview. Interviews are becoming far more structured than they were only a few years ago. Smart interviewers (and the growing numbers of lawsuits are waking up more of them every day) make sure they ask you only questions that relate to the skills needed to perform the duties of the position for which you are applying. Other questions can provide evidence of prejudice.

As a result, your interviewer will likely have a written list of questions, which will be followed like a director follows a movie script. The safest approach for interviewers is to ask the same questions of all applicants. Most interviewers will stay clear of casual comments or friendly chat, since unexpected comments during ice-breaking time can lead to discrimination lawsuits.

And don't be surprised if your prospective employer takes lots of notes during the interview. These notes are meant to protect the company in case you decide to sue. It provides a paper trail of just what each party says.

As a job applicant, you have a level of responsibility equal to that of the interviewer. If the courts protect you against discrimination, you should go half way by conducting yourself in a professional manner. Be smart. Don't volunteer information about your children, marital status, religion, or charity work, or anything else that does not relate to the job. Remember, bringing up personal information may damage your interview and could be embarrassing. At the very least, the interviewer will get the idea that you are unaware of all of the controversies surrounding employment lawsuits in recent years. And what employer wants an unaware employee? At worst, the employer may think you are trying to entrap the company in a lawsuit. Neither condition makes for a very satisfactory employer–worker relationship.

HOW TO HANDLE ILLEGAL QUESTIONS

What should you do during your job interview if you are confronted with what appears to be discriminatory questions? Let's take a look at your options.

> **Option 1. Become angry and accuse the interviewer of discrimination.** For many people this will be the automatic response. While the reaction is understandable, it's difficult to see any benefit to the applicant. Getting angry at the interviewer will bring the meeting to an end, and you won't get the job.

And there is another danger of which you should be aware: employers are allowed to discriminate if they can show that a characteristic, which is otherwise protected, is necessary for the employee to fulfill the duties required by the position. In other words, the employer may have a ready response to your charge of illegal discrimination. And you will be very embarrassed.

You want to give the interviewer the chance to explain how the offending question actually does relate to the essential duties of the job. That leads us to the next two options.

Option 2. Answer the questions as straightforwardly as you can. Here, you allow the interviewer to keep control of the discussion. You simply answer the questions as truthfully as you can. This option has the advantage of keeping you in the good graces of the interviewer.

The downside is that there may in fact be information that you do not want the interviewer to know. For example, you may be taking care of an elderly father who is disabled, and you figure this may cause some minor scheduling problems once you are aboard the company. And you also figure—probably rightly—that knowledge of this will work against you when it comes time to decide who to hire.

Option 3. Plead ignorance and ask what the question has to do with the job. For this one, you pause briefly while giving the question thought and say something like, "I'm not sure what that has to do with my ability to perform the work required by the position. Could you fill me in?" Try to say this without any malice, with a straight face, and with a tone of voice that reflects genuine interest.

A savvy interviewer will either withdraw the question or surprise you with an answer that shows the question's relevance to the job. A bigoted or uninformed interviewer will charge full speed ahead over the nearest cliff.

Whichever option you choose, remember this: None of the options keeps you from taking legal action against the employer if you truly believe that you have been victimized by discrimination. If this is the case, be sure to write down exactly what happened, in as much detail as possible, as soon as you can after the interview. You will need these written notes to show to an attorney.

You can locate an employment attorney by calling the bar association for your state. Each state association has a list of lawyers categorized by specialty.

CHAPTER EIGHT

Follow-up After an Interview

THANK YOU LETTERS

You've returned home from the interview. Things went very well, you thought. Now, all you can do is wait anxiously for a telephone call with a job offer or other news. The die is cast, the deed is done; there's nothing more you can do but wait.

Wrong.

Instead of passively waiting by the phone, you must initiate steps to advance your candidacy. This is the role of the thank you letter. You send a thank you letter to the interviewer expressing appreciation for the interviewer's taking time from a busy schedule to meet you, restating your qualifications, and repeating your interest and eagerness for the job. You can even volunteer relevant information not mentioned at the interview. For example, you forgot to mention you are teaching (or taking) evening classes in a specialized area relating to the job, you just learned something new about the job particularly suitable to your background, or you chair a trade association committee working on an issue of interest to the interviewer. You can also send a clipping of a recent trade magazine article you wrote on an issue of interest relating to the job to pique the interviewer's interest.

If there was a misconception in the interview—or the interviewer feels you are deficient in a certain area—now is the time to clear it up. For example, perhaps you are perceived as being overqualified, lack the educational background other candidates have, or have never worked

129

as a marketing manager in a specific industry before, although you have in other industries.

If you agreed to specific follow-up steps at a later time, mention them—for example, "I look forward to meeting Tim Donald, the regional sales manager, on Thursday," or "I will hand-deliver more samples of travel brochures and hotel press kits I have written to you tomorrow, as discussed." Indicate your eagerness for a next step, if none was discussed, to move the process along: "I will call you a week from tomorrow to see if a hiring decision has been made." Or perhaps "I have taken the liberty of preparing a proposal on how I would conduct training seminars for your junior accountants and would be happy to discuss it with you. Would Monday be a good day for you?" Another take-charge approach: "I would be delighted to meet with you after you finish interviewing other candidates to discuss new issues which have arisen."

WHEN TO SEND THANK YOU LETTERS

Always send a thank you letter after each interview. Do it as soon as possible—the next day, or at least within the next few days—since the interviewer's memory is likely to cloud over after seeing dozens of applicants. Be sure to send the letter to everyone who had a role in interviewing you, even if you were in a group interview with six people. Surprisingly, many people who automatically write thank you notes for personal reasons—after a wedding gift or a weekend in the country—neglect their manners when it comes to job interviewing. Think of the interviewer as dangling the chance of a $40,000 (or $75,000, or whatever) gift before your eyes—it may just whet your appetite to sit down and compose that letter.

LETTER FORMAT

The letter should be short (one page or less), direct, personalized, mirror the tone of the interview (formal vs. casual), and match your qualifications against the requirements of the job in a reader-friendly way. (If it's not personalized, you defeat the whole purpose in sending the letter. Don't insult the interviewer by making him or her feel indistinguishable from a crowd.) It should be typed, not handwritten, on personal stationery or fine-quality white or cream bond paper, letter-sized or somewhat smaller. Leave artsy notecards, cute stationery, wild colors, and flourished handwriting for close friends and relatives.

Objectives of thank you letters

- Thank the interviewer for his or her time, demonstrating that you have good manners.
- Remind the interviewer who you are, when you met, and which position you are applying for.
- Highlight your qualifications and accomplishments.
- Overcome any obstacle raised in the interview (lack of experience, lack of educational degrees, etc.).
- Add new information which may open up another line of discussion and distinguish you from other job-seekers.
- State your interest in and enthusiasm for the job and how you believe you can make a positive contribution.
- Mention the next step if stated, or take the lead and suggest one.

Interviewers say a follow-up letter by itself is not enough to change the outcome of an interview—it won't make or break a situation—but among candidates who are roughly equal in qualifications, it may be the "icing on the cake" that inclines the interviewer to look favorably upon you.

Use the two sample follow-up letters on pages 132 and 133 as a guide.

KEEPING TRACK OF INTERVIEWS

It's important to keep track of your interviews and your follow-up in some organized fashion. Short-term memory fades very rapidly, so you've got to put down your thoughts on paper quickly. Start by taking notes during the interview itself and add to them on your ride home if you take the train or bus. Write down the name and title of the interviewer, key issues discussed during the interview, what the interviewer intends to solve by filling the position, obstacles to hiring you (whether expressed or not), additional people who participated in the interview, who seems to be the decision maker, etc.

You should also rate your interest in the job. Borrow a page from restaurant reviewers and give four stars if you would practically die

Katherine Marin
72 Barrow Street
New York, N.Y. 10014

September 5, 1995

Mr. Alan Heller
Senior Vice President
The Robinson Group
155 Fifth Avenue
New York, N.Y. 10010

Dear Mr. Heller:

Thank you so much for taking the time to see me yesterday for the position of Vice President/Account Supervisor in your travel group.

As Vice President of MLA Associates, a Los Angeles-based public relations agency specializing in the travel industry, I managed a campaign to launch the new Globe Hotel in Las Vegas which resulted in TV, print, and radio placements in 35 countries, receptions to introduce the hotel to travel agents and meeting planners, and special promotions which led to the booking of 10,000 rooms in the hotel's first two months. The campaign won a Public Relations Society of America Gold Anvil award as the most innovative travel campaign of 1994.

I am excited about the opportunity to make a contribution to the accounts in your travel group, including supervising the launch of two new hotels in Beverly Hills and Chicago which you mentioned.

I'll call you a week from tomorrow to see if you have arrived at a hiring decision.

Again, I appreciate the chance to meet with you.

Cordially,

Katherine Marin

John Haywood
515 East Holland Avenue
Carol Steam, IL 60188

May 16, 1995

Mr. Lawrence Mann
Vice President
Bentsen & Lawson
25 Michigan Avenue
Chicago, IL 60604

Dear Mr. Mann:

I greatly appreciated the chance to meet you today for the position of Manager of Training and Development.

I believe I am well suited for the position, which requires at least five years of experience in training and development at another accounting firm. During my eight years at Tibbett & Eastwood, I conducted sales training for individual teams, led internal focus groups, and conducted surveys. I also worked closely with top management in developing change management seminars, which I understand your firm is particularly interested in implementing.

I am writing a proposal for training and developing your staff which I will hand-deliver to your office on Friday. I would be happy to discuss it with you, if you like.

Thank you for taking the time to meet with me.

Cordially,

John Haywood

Interview Record

Name of Company:

Address: Phone:

Industry:

Interviewer: Title:

Position Applied For:

Date:

Key Issues:

Follow-up Note Mailed:

Additional Follow-up:

Job Lead Obtained From:

Additional Person Spoken To:

Comments:

My Interest In Job:

happy if you won the job, three stars for great delight, two stars for fair interest, and one star for minimal interest.

Follow the interview record sample on page 134. Index cards or sheets of paper can be used if you prefer. Just keep them in a box or folder, categorized alphabetically for easy reference. Keep referring to and updating the cards as you send follow-up letters, obtain new interviews, and so on.

TELEPHONE FOLLOW-UP

On some occasions, a follow-up telephone call is acceptable. For example, after sending your thank you letter, you want to know where you stand with the company because you have received another job offer. Or you have vital new information you want the interviewer to receive in a timely fashion. Let's say you've just been promoted or the department you head has just won an award for quality control. Perhaps you've thought further about the specific marketing problem the interviewer raised and had a brainstorm you'd like to put into a proposal.

At any rate, don't be a telephone pest. Be short, sweet, and try to anticipate questions before the interviewer asks them. For example, call and say: "Mr. Swenson? This is Marie Simmons. We met on May 2 to discuss the account executive opening. I've just gotten a job offer from ABC Advertising. Since I'm very interested in working for your firm— and have experience in working on consumer products accounts—I was curious as to whether a hiring decision has been made."

COPING WITH REJECTION

By the way, if you have been rejected for a job, don't think all hope is lost. As the cliché goes, "It ain't over till the fat lady sings." When you are rejected through a telephone call—or by letter—ask the interviewer the reason why. Listen very carefully—without arguing each point or being defensive—and take notes. Like it or not, these comments are the negative perceptions that shot down your candidacy. When the interviewer finishes explaining the reason to you, ask politely and enthusiastically for the chance at a second interview to address these points.

More often than you would think, the interviewer—impressed by your gutsiness and tenacity in the face of rejection—will say yes. If this happens, outdo yourself in preparing to overcome the objections that have been handed to you on a silver platter, regardless of whether or not you agree with them. (It's irrelevant.) Brush up on your knowledge of a specific subject area, or be more proactive, or talk more slowly— whatever the objections are. Send a follow-up letter afterward, thanking the interviewer for a second chance. If you get the job after this, heartily congratulate yourself—through your own persuasiveness and force of character, you have succeeded.

CHAPTER NINE

How to Negotiate and Evaluate Job Offers

After months of unemployment and looking for a job, you finally get a job offer. Your gratitude is boundless: you leap to your feet, warmly clasp the interviewer's hand, and cry: "Yes! I accept your offer and will start May 1."

Resist the impulse. You may be doing yourself a disservice by forfeiting thousands of dollars in annual salary, missing out on key employee benefits, and making the wrong move for your career.

Keep a cool head. Thomas Jefferson once said, "Nothing gives a person so much advantage over another as to remain always cool and unruffled under all circumstances." The wisest approach is to express warm interest at the offer, say you need a little time to think about it, go home, and start evaluating and analyzing in earnest.

You should evaluate your job offer in three main areas:

- Salary, including benefits and perks
- Position
- Company

Let's start with the hardest first.

SALARY

The key to successful negotiation is to produce an outcome that is beneficial to both sides. In a win-win negotiation, each side sees the other as an ally—not an adversary—and seeks a creative solution to defeat a problem, not each other.

According to one of the classics on negotiation, *You Can Negotiate Anything* by Herb Cohen, the game plan for win-win negotiations has these elements:

- Establishing trust
- Obtaining information
- Meeting the other's needs
- Using the other's ideas
- Transforming the relationship into collaboration
- Taking moderate risk
- Getting the other's help

Let's apply these principles to a job interview. Face facts: The employer wants to hire someone for as little money as possible, while the job-seeker wants as much money as possible. However, in order to bridge this abyss, the job-seeker should empathize with the interviewer's needs, be cooperative, ask questions, and pool ideas, information, and experience in an atmosphere of mutual trust to solve a common problem: salary. In other words, see "where the interviewer is coming from" to arrive at a mutually satisfactory conclusion. Don't arbitrarily ask for an unrealistic figure, then dig in your heels and refuse to budge. Don't make the mistake many people make in negotiating:

> . . . they begin negotiating with an opponent by announcing *their* alternative or answer. They may even take a harder line and express *their* conclusion as a demand or ultimatum. Being confronted by your opponent's position, usually stated numerically, causes you to respond in kind. Suddenly, both sides are poles apart in a competitive win-lose negotiating mode. The potential ally has suddenly become an adversary.
>
> (from *You Can Negotiate Anything* by Herb Cohen)

For example, the interviewer asks you to name the salary you want. You say $43,000. The interviewer says, "That's a little high for us. We only intend to pay $35,000 for the position." You retort: "Well, I still want $43,000 and I'm not willing to go any lower." The interviewer: "Good-bye, and thank you for coming." End of interview. You complain to your family or friends that night: "It was impossible. He wouldn't budge an inch. He refused to negotiate."

How different the outcome might have been if the following scenario had taken place:

In response to the interviewer's question about your desired salary, you could have stalled a bit, said something like: "I just want to make sure I've gotten all the responsibilities of the job straight," and enumerated them. You then could have followed with the time-honored art of answering a question with a question, and inquired: "Have I left anything out?" or "Does this accurately reflect the job at hand?" After both of you had reached a mutual understanding of the job, you could have asked the interviewer: "What salary range is authorized for the position?" Or perhaps inquired what salary range—not salary figure, in order to leave room for negotiation—a person with your background and skills could expect. Upon hearing the range was $35,000–$40,000, depending upon experience, you could have piggybacked onto the higher range and offered a reason to justify it, countering, politely and smoothly: "We're pretty close—I'm seeking a range of $38,000–$45,000, due to my experience in writing and editing in-house newsletters in your industry. How flexible is your upper salary range?"

An alternative: "Let's talk about this. I'm looking for a minimum salary of $38,000 and a maximum of $45,000, based upon my extensive experience in this field. But I know I can make a real contribution launching a newsletter for your firm and am sure we can work things out."

Because you are not being inflexible—you are signaling your respect for the interviewer's needs and willingness to reach a mutually agreeable solution, while demonstrating your qualifications for the job—it is very likely the interviewer may restate the offer in the upper salary range.

If not—let's say the interviewer only wants to rise to $38,000 or thinks your qualifications are worth only $35,000—consider asking to make up the difference in benefits and perks (see below). Think of them as simply money in another form, and as a more palatable way for the employer to sweeten your compensation. Some will be more important to you than others, depending on your and your family's needs. While certain benefits are very valuable—such as pension, 401K and profit-sharing plans, medical and dental insurance with low deductibles and extensive coverage—others are more status- and comfort-oriented, such as health-club and country-club memberships.

BENEFITS AND PERKS

A benefits package can often be worth anywhere from 20% to 40% of your salary. In addition, some benefits are not taxed as income, in contrast to your salary. At some companies, all employees receive certain benefits. However, the higher your position, the easier it will be for you to negotiate more benefits and perks. As with everything in life, if you don't ask, you often don't receive. Also be aware that benefit packages vary widely in different industries. Fortune 500 companies tend to have generous packages.

Some or all of the following benefits may be brought up with a job offer:

- "Cafeteria-style" flexible insurance plans (employees are allowed to design plans which best meet their needs)
- Medical insurance (some companies have much lower deductibles and a higher proportion which is company-paid than others; some cover psychotherapy, vision plans, pregnancy, and dependents)
- Dental insurance (less common than medical insurance; some companies have lower deductibles and a higher company-paid proportion)
- Pension or 401K plans (These plans vary a good deal; find out about vesting policies and how long you must be employed before you can contribute. In 401K plans, your employer may match a certain percentage of a pre-tax contribution from your salary.)
- Profit sharing (a less common but very desirable benefit)
- Disability insurance (see how the company defines disability, the salary cutoff point where a lower percentage of your salary is paid, and if short-term disability is available)
- Vacation (one to two weeks per full year of employment is standard for new employees)
- Paid sick leave (one to two weeks of sick leave and personal days is standard for new employees)
- Personal days
- Life insurance (a very common benefit; supplemental coverage—which offers much more coverage than the small amount generally offered by companies—is usually available as well)
- Child care (day-care centers are on-site at some companies; others reimburse child care expenses)
- Parental leave (some companies offer paid leave to both parents)
- Counseling services (these include drug- or alcohol-abuse, retirement, financial, outplacement counseling, and legal services)
- Educational reimbursement (some companies pay all or a portion of job-related classes or degree programs; some have internal training programs)
- Nursing home and long-term home care (some companies pay premiums; at others, you pay but obtain group rates)
- Stock options (at public companies usually for management-level employees)
- Employment and/or termination contract
- Company car
- Car allowance, insurance, or gas and maintenance
- Health-club or country-club membership
- Expense account
- Administrative assistant
- Designated parking space

Another suggestion to improve the situation if the employer fails to meet your salary requirement: try to increase your future salary. For example, perhaps you can convince the employer to agree to a promotion and raise after three months or so. Or you may want to negotiate at least a performance review with a raise after a certain time period. A year-end bonus, based on good performance, of course, or a lump-sum signing bonus upon taking the job can also be negotiated.

TIPS FOR SALARY AND BENEFITS NEGOTIATION

1. **Negotiate from a position of strength.** You are never going to be in a more desirable position than you are right now, after a job offer has been made—and before you accept it. The employer wants you; the employer is not sure he or she can have you; the timing is perfect. All's right with the world. Realize your power and seize the moment. Push for the salary and benefits package you desire—later is too late.

2. **Postpone all discussion of salary until you receive an offer.** The tactful way to respond to prematurely posed questions such as "What kind of salary are you looking for?" is to say something like "I'd really like to know more about the position and its responsibilities before we talk about salary." After all, how can you possibly figure out what salary would be appropriate unless the job is defined for you? Draw the interviewer out more about the job and the specific problems that need to be solved in the company. If the interviewer is very persistent, and you feel backed against a wall, answer in terms of a salary range, not a fixed amount.

3. **Whoever mentions salary first, loses.** You box yourself in if you mention the salary you want first. You can conceivably lose two ways: citing a salary lower than you could get, or higher than what the employer is willing to pay. Let the interviewer be the first to announce a figure.

4. **Assertiveness in salary negotiation is rewarded.** If you don't ask for a higher salary, benefits, or perks, you won't get them. Your chances are best if you ask for no more than 25% above the highest amount the interviewer has mentioned. Even if the interviewer offers a salary that is fine by you, still try to win a 10% to 20% increase. If you win, you really win, but even if you lose, you win. However, remember to cite a reason why you deserve a certain

salary or package to soften the blow, so the interviewer can justify the offer to upper management. The worst that can happen is that you may be turned down on specific requests. The offer, however, will not be withdrawn as long as you show flexibility and a willingness to cooperate.

5. **Anything is negotiable.** This includes salary, future salary (promotion with raise within a certain timeframe, performance review with raise), signing bonus or annual bonus, benefits and perks, title, and responsibilities of the job itself. For lower positions, there is less room for negotiation. Such jobs are not that valuable to the bottom line, and there may be a great deal of competition for the position, particularly in "glamour" industries like entertainment, public relations, and book publishing. Often, for lower- and middle-management positions, you can expect 10%–20% more than the salary offered to you.

6. **Decide the salary you want and be prepared to justify it.** Figure out a range, with the low point being the market rate for your skills and experience and the high point being a generous salary for comparable jobs in the industry. It's very important to know the market rate for your skills and experience. You can do this by reading salary surveys in magazines, newspapers (such as the *National Business Employment Weekly*), and trade publications, by speaking with executive recruiters and networking contacts, and by scanning help wanted ads and statistics on occupations from the U.S. Bureau of Labor Statistics. Salary negotiations cannot be made in a vacuum. If you are a woman, automatically assume you are underpaid, and tack on another 20%–30% to your current salary in forming your desired salary.

7. **Experience matters.** Understand that most if not all jobs have salary ranges. If you can demonstrate a high level of competence and/or experience, you can justify asking for a somewhat higher salary than the market rate.

8. **Negotiating down is much easier than negotiating up.** Once you box yourself in by mentioning a low salary, it is difficult to get a higher one. Place yourself in the infinitely happier position of working your way down from a generous salary to one that is market rate at minimum. If the interviewer offers a salary range lower than what you expect, counter with a range starting slightly below the high part of the interviewer's range.

9. **Always talk in terms of salary ranges, not flat amounts.** Flat amounts are perceived as confrontational and often tend to end the

dialogue. Remember, as a win-win negotiator, leave some room to satisfy both your needs and the interviewer's.

10. **When asked for your minimum salary requirement, cite the low point of your salary range.** This means the market-rate salary for your skills/experience, not your bare-bones subsistence level, or your current (or past) salary.

11. **Don't accept or reject an offer as soon as it is offered.** Accepting on the spot makes you seem too eager, and probably means that you are cheating yourself on the salary and benefits package. Be interested and noncommittal, and ask for a few days—or, at the very least, overnight—to think about it. Employers expect this, and, besides, you need to weigh the job, title, salary, and benefits package. It's generally not a good sign if the interviewer urges you to make an immediate decision. Read some trade publications or talk to people knowledgeable about the company to see if there are problems or an especially high turnover rate. Exceptions are lower-level positions in "glamour" and other very competitive industries, and entrepreneurially driven firms, which operate at a much higher speed than other companies. Try for at least *some* "think" time, however—whatever the job offer.

12. **List the pros and cons of the job.** Take a piece of paper and write down all the positive and negative aspects of the job, company, and salary and benefits package. Possibly, you may have other competing job offers to weigh as well. Decide the factors which are very important to you, as well as the ones you are willing to compromise on. For example, a relatively low-paying position in television—an industry that truly excites you—may be more valuable in your eyes than a higher-paying position in an industry which does not. Or medical and dental benefits may not be a factor if you are covered by your spouse's benefits. All things are not equal to different people.

13. **Always allow the interviewer to "save face."** Be polite but firm—the iron hand in the velvet glove. Place yourself within the mind-set of the interviewer—realize that if the interviewer is going to rise from his or her offered salary of $40,000 to the $48,000 you desire, he or she will need a pretty good reason to do so. Make it easy for the interviewer to justify this substantial increase to upper management, and still feel like a winner in the negotiation.

14. **If the employer fails to meet your salary requirement, try to increase your future salary.** For example, perhaps you can convince the employer to agree to a promotion and raise after

three months on the job. Or you may want to negotiate at least a performance review with a raise after a certain time period. A year-end bonus, based on good performance, of course, or a lump-sum signing bonus upon taking the job can also be negotiated.

15. **Upgrade a job to a higher-level position to justify a higher salary.** Jobs and titles can be reshaped and redefined as well as salaries. For example, a salary which may be out of line and against company policy for a senior account executive position in a public relations agency may be just fine for a vice president slot. An office manager may have one salary; a vice president of operations position will pay considerably more, yet encompass many of the same functions. Demonstrate that you deserve the higher title and more responsible job and chances are the higher salary will follow.

16. **When you accept an offer, spell out the terms.** To avoid uncomfortable misunderstandings when your job begins, repeat the terms, as you understand them, to the interviewer. "Let's see if we agree on everything: I will accept the position as associate account manager for the consumer products group at $60,000, and can start June 1. My benefits will include the right to hire my own assistant, a company car with gas and mileage allowance, and a profit-sharing and 401K plan."

17. **Don't burn your bridges.** Write a cordial resignation letter to your current boss, hand it in, and discuss the situation cordially. Give adequate notice so a replacement can be found. Inform other firms who extended job offers and executive recruiters with whom you are working that you have found a position. Thank them profusely, and say you would like to keep the lines of communication open. You never know when you may need to look for another job.

18. **Ask for the offer in writing.** Far better to have the protection of a written offer than to quit your job, only to find that the verbal offer from your presumed employer-to-be has vanished like smoke.

19. **The more easily you can walk away from the offer, the stronger your negotiating position.** Again, like courtship, the person with the greater need and emotional investment is in the weaker position. If you don't want or need the job that much, you'll want a higher salary to compensate for your less-than-warm attitude.

20. **Look at the whole package, not just salary.** Looking at the salary alone can be deceptive. Factor in the dollar value of a

generous benefits package—such as profit-sharing and 401K plans, medical and dental plans with low deductibles, paid maternity leave, expense account, four-week vacation—and you will see they can easily add tens of thousands of dollars to your salary. A $28,000 job with $20,000 worth of benefits may be more valuable to you than a $35,000 job with $5,000 in benefits—if these are benefits you and your family need. Best of all, some benefits are not taxed.

21. **Leverage job offers.** Contact other companies you have interviewed with as soon as you get a job offer, not just out of courtesy. Call to say that you have just received a job offer but are still interested in meeting them again in the very near future. This may very well increase their interest in you; everyone wants a "hot property." Try to leverage your single job offer into several, which makes it easier to evaluate the original offer.

22. **Don't just accept the first offer which comes along.** First, try to have several interviews you're interested in going on in the same time span. This is best accomplished through a full and intense job search plan. Second, realize there will be other interviews—and that there is freelancing, tempwork, and other options. Building self-esteem will prevent you from making an unwise decision.

HOW TO EVALUATE THE JOB

It's wise not to make a premature decision to grab the job before you investigate further. Yet many people do, seduced by what they hear on the grapevine about the company. Ask the interviewer for a job description and listen very carefully to what is said.

Beforehand, take a piece of paper and list the things you want out of a job, in terms of both material and intangible rewards. Divide these into things you *must* have and those you would merely *like* to have. For some people, frequent business travel to other parts of the United States or abroad is a real delight; others dislike it. Frequent client contact can be a real plus to some job-seekers; you may prefer a more behind-the-scenes role. Attendance at lots of dinners and parties may be tedious or a perk of the job, depending on the person. After the job is offered to you, match your desires against the job itself.

Figure out if the job is a good choice for your career track. Will you be learning more and progressing faster than if you remained at your current firm? However, if you are a career-changer—either by choice or by such factors as downsizing or plant closure—recognize a relatively low-paying, low-level job may be a fact of life.

Find out what happened to your predecessor in the position. Ask if you can talk to employees. You can learn very helpful things—such as four people held the position in the past two years and were terminated. Some companies are not for the timid and while a sink-or-swim, pressure-cooker atmosphere may be fine for you, it's nice to know ahead of time.

HOW TO EVALUATE THE COMPANY

Read about the company in business publications, trade magazines, business directories like *Standard & Poor's* and *Moody's Manuals*, and annual reports. You should have already researched the firm before the interview. Talk to people who know about the firm—from executive recruiters who may have gotten you the interview to employees at the firm to competitors at other firms.

Then, assess the company, its health and growth. Also assess the corporate culture and see if it matches your temperament and values. Working in a bureaucratic environment is fine for some people. Others prefer the challenge and style of a fast-paced entrepreneurial atmosphere. Still others prefer a casual or creative environment. By all means, try to find out if the company's culture suits you. A prestigious title and high salary may not be worth it if your job satisfaction plummets and your health breaks down. (If you think it's worth it, best of luck.)

Assess your future boss' style and see if it is compatible with your own. It doesn't bode well if you like the company but can't stand your boss.

CHAPTER TEN

If You're 40+: Advice to Older Job-Seekers

TODAY'S OLDER WORKFORCE

The "graying" of the American workforce is at hand. By the year 2000, the median age of employees in the U.S. will be nearly 40. Fifty-one percent of all workers will be age 35 to 54, while 11% to 13% will be over 55. In fact, workers 55-plus are the fastest-growing sector of the workforce—their numbers are expected to jump 38% by the year 2005, according to the Bureau of Labor Statistics.

Older workers are also out looking for work in droves—whether laid off in disproportionately high numbers from corporate downsizing, making midlife career switches, chasing after better opportunities, or returning to the labor force after a hiatus.

In many cases, unfortunately, interviewers are reluctant to hire 40+ job applicants because they fear the person may think or act "old"—be out of touch with the times and industry trends, be rigid or inflexible in thinking and behavior, and so on. "You can't teach an old dog new tricks" is a cliché believed by many in our youth-obsessed society. If are in the 40+ category, the best way to counteract prejudice is to emphasize the unique advantages your age brings to the job you are seeking.

You must remove any mental roadblocks you possess that prevent you from getting the position you want. If you think "old" and believe you won't find a job again, don't be surprised if you don't. You've already turned yourself down—why shouldn't others? On the other hand, if you radiate confidence, the results will usually be positive.

PLUSES OF OLDER WORKERS

Let's look at the pluses of your age and how to highlight them in job interviews. Then, we'll tackle the negative stereotypes interviewers may hold and how to dispel them.

Wealth of contacts. Twenty or 30 years of contacts in an industry sure beats having 2—or 5 or 10. Take advantage of the many contacts you've made over the years—from colleagues to clients to suppliers to competitors—they're your own private treasure trove for networking to generate job interviews. (See Chapter 1 for more on networking and Chapter 4 for how to conduct informational interviews with network contacts.)

Experience and knowledge. You have priceless inside know-how about how your industry has operated and changed over the years, which is superior to the book knowledge of recently minted MBAs. Even more important, you are seasoned at dealing with many situations and individuals. You have already learned from past mistakes.

Managerial experience. You probably have skills in supervising, motivating, and mentoring other workers, unlike many younger job-seekers.

Reliability, loyalty, and trustworthiness. Many older workers have a strong work ethic and a high level of motivation, qualities often lacking in younger employees. A report by the Conference Board, "Job Banks for Retirees," on companies that have job banks for retirees, says the Travelers Corporation, the insurance and financial services giant, found older workers less likely to stay home in bad weather than other workers. Digital Equipment Corporation never had discipline or attendance problems with older employees. The report found that even when older and younger workers possessed equivalent skills, older workers were much more reliable and loyal.

Job dedication. Because older workers are often less eager to be on the career fast track than ambitious younger workers, they are apt to pay more attention to the demands of the job itself, and are not perceived as a threat.

Flexibility in working. Since older workers usually do not have young children and have fewer demands on their time, they often are more flexible about work hours, and willing to work late and on weekends.

OVERCOMING NEGATIVE STEREOTYPES

Stereotypes about older workers die hard. A study of 1,000 managers in different businesses by the American Association of Retired Persons (AARP) and the Society of Human Resource Management found that while workers age 50+ are admired for their reliable work habits and skills, they are undervalued and underutilized.

Martin Sicker, director of Work Force Programs for the AARP, notes that older workers are often lumped together in a category by employers in a way younger workers are not, which ignores the diversity of their skills and backgrounds. "Everybody sees them as being like a Saint Bernard," he laments.

Here are some tips for overcoming these negative stereotypes at your interview:

Show enthusiasm. Act energetic, alert, and enthusiastic—the type of person they want to hire. Make your eyes sparkle, your handshake firm, and your tone of voice brisk and lively. Sit forward in your seat to show eagerness. "The key to going into the interview is to be totally energized but to express that in a positive charged way—so your energy level seems consistent with that of younger people," says Nancy Josephs, president of Brookshire Enterprises, a New York career development firm. "Use high-energy words—and cite hobbies that show energy, like skiing, or bicycle riding," advises Kate Wendleton, founder of The Five O'Clock Club, a national job search strategy group.

Dress sharp. Dress and look "sharp," as people often make the leap that those who look "old-fashioned" will be equally stodgy in their thinking. Make sure your clothing is stylish and flattering. You don't have to seize onto the latest fashion trend, but look reasonably "with it."

Demonstrate current skills. Go out of your way to demonstrate that your skills are current and that you are knowledgeable about current trends your industry. Mention your computer literacy, your knowledge of Japanese, Russian, or French—even though these are on your résumé. A 1992 survey by Louis Harris & Associates of 3,000 people age 50+ who are willing to work but are unemployed found that older workers are more flexible about working conditions than is generally assumed. Sixty percent of those surveyed were willing to accept a lower salary than their last job, 72% were willing to work alone, 84% to work two or three days a week, and 41% to stand up most of the day.

Ability to work well with younger people. Demonstrate that you are comfortable with being interviewed by a younger person, with working along with many younger people, and with the prospect that your boss may be younger as well. Don't display uneasiness verbally or through body language—at any of these possibilities.

INTERVIEW QUESTIONS

Let's review some typical interview questions and statements older job seekers may face, what they mean, and how to deal with them:

Q. "How old are you (Or "What year did you graduate from high school or college?")

Meaning: You're too old for us.

Your response: These are illegal questions; you don't have to answer them. (See Chapter 7 for more information about illegal interview questions.) Nevertheless, don't win the battle and lose the war. Being confrontational, telling the interviewer off for violating the law, and storming out will not win you the job. A more prudent course is to ask if age is a concern; if the response is yes, point out how your qualifications match the job at hand, and how 25 years in a changing field have made you adaptable in meeting new and varied challenges.

Q. "Your résumé (background, qualifications, etc.) is certainly impressive."

Meaning: You're overqualified.

Your response: Address the real concerns of the interviewer, who worries you may be dissatisfied and/or unproductive in a position you feel is "beneath" you. Or that you will take the position as a stop-gap measure until the first golden opportunity comes along. Say something like: "If you think I'm overqualified, I'd like to point out that my experience in developing new overseas markets and my specific skills in product promotion make a perfect fit for the position you have open." Explain how your experience can impact the company's bottom line and lessen training time for you, and offer reasons why the position presents challenges you welcome.

Q. "What years were you employed at these companies?"

Meaning: A sneaky way of guessing how old you are.

Your response: Answer the question, since the interviewer will be able to verify the dates with your ex-employers anyway. Redirect the question from your past to the present. Point out how your job history shows reliability, and how your experience and skills are of value to this specific company in the particular position open.

Q. "We try to be on the cutting edge, and have a lot of young people on staff. How do you feel about that?"

Meaning: You won't fit in (or: You're too old-fashioned for us).

Your response: Explain how forward-thinking your career has been, in terms of new technologies you have mastered or recent challenges you have met. Assuage your interviewer's concern by noting that you welcome working with—and mentoring—young people, and have done so in the past.

Q. "Do you mind working for a younger boss?"

Meaning: You're going to resent it, be condescending, and difficult to deal with.

Your response: Above all, don't look uncomfortable at the possibility. Say that you tend to work well with your superiors regardless of their age. (Remember, this is not the time to exhibit any bias on your part.) Cite examples where you have worked well for younger bosses, or with younger colleagues, at the office or in outside organizations.

Q. **"We don't want people with a 9-to-5 mentality here. Is that a problem?"**

Meaning: You won't want to work long hours and don't have enough energy.

Your response: Explain that you have a devotion to the job that needs to be done, and fully understand that it may spill into after hours. Note that you often come in early, or leave late (or both), and that job reviews have always noted your productivity. Explain that you have more energy to channel into your work since you have fewer distractions than many younger people.

CAREER STRATEGIES

Career experts advise older workers to follow these strategies:

Target smaller businesses or high-growth industries.

Large companies, even profitable ones, have been going through tremendous downsizings. Most job growth is in smaller businesses. Sometimes, seeking work in a "trendy" area of a field you are already working in produces results.

A 42-year-old oil exploration geologist, who found oil for three companies in the course of his career, couldn't strike oil in the job market, to his chagrin. After heeding advice to take classes in environmental geology due to the growing "green" (ecologically friendly) movement, he landed a job in this field for a foreign-owned corporation in Texas, according to Leon Leidner, chairman of the Queens, New York, office of SCORE (Service Corps of Retired Executives), a program sponsored by the U.S. Small Business Administration where retired executives counsel people starting their own businesses and job-hunters.

"You contaminated the earth, now you can uncontaminate it," Mr. Leidner recalls telling him.

Upgrade your skills—and acquire new skills.

This makes you much more marketable. Going back to school—to learn new skills, brush up on rusty skills, or even pursue a degree—can pay off for several reasons. Certain skills, such as computer literacy, may be essential in your field, and you will considered flawed without them. Other skills, such as foreign languages or knowledge of statistics, may be desirable but not essential, and having them may help package you as a competent job candidate. Career planning workshops may be helpful if you want to change careers, identify your talents and interests, focus your goals, learn job-hunting and interview techniques, or get overviews of specific careers. Business and graduate school preparation courses are available if you want to pursue a master's degree. Networking opportunities also abound—with the teacher, with other students, and so on.

The inexpensive adult education classes offered by many colleges in the evening, on weekends, and during the day are an excellent resource. YMCAs, YMHAs, and some high schools also hold classes for adults. Some also offer one-on-one career counseling, vocational testing, and extensive career resource files. A quick read of their catalogues will reveal a wealth of possibilities, ranging from workshops to one-day seminars to weekly classes.

Thanks to a New York University School of Continuing Education career change workshop, Alan Friedman switched gears midlife from corporate attorney with J.C. Penney and his family's law firm to entrepreneur, starting a placement agency for nannies. Mr. Friedman says he is enjoying himself and working much harder than he ever did as an attorney.

Mr. Leidner of SCORE, after retiring as chief executive officer of a men's clothing manufacturer and mail order company in 1987, went to get his MBA (and was mistaken by a security guard as faculty). "Don't be discouraged—there's a whole world out there," he says. "Never close your mind—keep it open at all times."

Exploit your network of contacts—keep up with old ones, and continually meet and cultivate new ones.

Ed Amira, who at age 50 was laid off from his job at a senior data communications analyst by a securities firm, credits The Five O'Clock Club with teaching him the importance of networking. Once a novice in this area, he notes he has been converted to a "true believer in networking." Surprised and pleased by the success he has garnered, he recalls that his first consulting assignment was landed thanks to a call to a business friend from 10 years ago. A job interview resulted from chatting with a man sitting next to him during outplacement sessions, who thought the job he had just interviewed for would be more suitable for Mr. Amira. "I'm amazed how many people remember you if you've been nice to them," Mr. Amira recalls. "Even people not in my field have given me leads."

Don't rest on past laurels—or think the world owes you a living.

Remember the adage heeded by many clients—what have you done for me this week? Think of the job interviewer as your client, in a sense—what can do you to satisfy their future needs? Overconfidence can be just as detrimental as lack of confidence. Taking a realistic look at the current job market and making an objective assessment of how you can fit into it are of critical importance. "Senior-level executives who have lost a job after reaching a certain level often think they can move right into another position and bypass getting back to basics," says Christopher Hunt, editor of *Workplace America*, a Greenwich, Connecticut–based newsletter. "They can be some of the most difficult people to interview." Talking to career counselors or human resources personnel can be helpful in gaining an overall perspective.

Expect the market range for your skills—not your past salary.

In the eyes of the job market, older executives are often seen as too expensive and may require retraining. Many years of experience in outmoded technologies can be outweighed by short experience in cutting-edge technologies. Be aware of these attitudes and don't allow yourself to be derailed by them.

Reposition yourself.

Sometimes the pain of the job search which can be worse than the pain of not having a job—can paralyze an applicant into inaction.

A 59-year-old former vice president of operations at a pharmaceutical company landed a job in 11 months with the same title, a higher salary, and closer to his home at a chemical company. However, the first few months after he was laid off he was "catatonic," recalls Barbara Barra, senior vice president of Lee Hecht Harrison, the third-largest outplacement firm in the United States. "He was so convinced he would never get a job again—he was immediately thinking about selling his house and moving from New Jersey, yet he couldn't get himself to conduct an active job search! He would come in every day to read the papers and make phone calls, and be gone by noon."

After a while, he became revitalized, and started networking—which he was reluctant to do before. He repositioned his résumé, away from his responsibilities to emphasize specific skills and accomplishments. For example, for the first time he included his position as project manager of a quality team that saved his company $1 million over two years—a fact he was too self-effacing to mention previously. Before, his résumé stated he oversaw warehouse distribution, which—while true—did not differentiate how his skills and abilities varied from anyone else holding the same position.

Show a confident, can-do attitude which demonstrates you can positively impact a company's bottom line.

This can do wonders to dispel age stereotypes. One truly inspiring success story: A salesman of condiments to restaurants, employed at the same firm for 40 years, was laid off when the firm was sold—without a pension or even severance. He found a sales job in two weeks—at age 81. Approaching a competitor, he said: "Don't pay me a cent—I'll work strictly on commission," Ms. Barra remembers.

Convert your former employer into a client.

A 56-year-old executive laid off from a chemical company found himself in the flattering—yet insulting—position of constantly receiving calls for information in his specialty from his ex-employer. Sell your information, Mr. Leidner advised. He did—and became a consultant with his ex-employer as his major client. He now earns in three days what he previously did in five days.

REVERSING THE TRENDS

After firing tens of thousands of employees and thinning out its middle management ranks, Corporate America is finding itself short of employees with depth and breadth of experience.

This is one reason why, over the past eight years, there has been a dramatic difference in the market perception of older workers—and less of an age issue than ever before, says Ms. Barra of Lee Hecht Harrison. Another reason is that companies are simply not thinking long-term anymore. They no longer expect to get 20–30 years of loyal service from any worker—young or old. This means that, in many cases, if you can demonstrate the skills to solve their problems on a short-term basis, this may outweigh your age, Ms. Barra notes.

The "Baby Boomer Glut" also has helped improve perceptions of older workers. The generation that didn't want to trust anyone over 30 is now over 30, graying, saddled with responsibilities, and accustomed to the idea of longer and multiple careers. Baby boomers are often in the interviewer's chair and are often worried about being downsized themselves. A recognition that "they" are now "us" can soften impressions since baby boomers are edging into the category of older workers themselves.

FORTY PLUS CLUBS

Forty Plus is a nationwide, nonprofit chain of job search and support groups which help unemployed executives and professionals over 40 who have earned at least $40,000 per year. Its 21 chapters maintain computerized job banks, which match members to job listings. Forty Plus does not charge a fee to employers or executive search firms. Training in interview and résumé-writing techniques, computer skills, job search strategy, and networking is offered. Members are carefully screened; references from six former employers and/or business associates are required and checked. Members are permitted to use the Forty Plus office and fax machines, telephones, and computers for their job hunts. Alumni who are employed assist unemployed members on a regular basis.

Fees vary by city. In some chapters, which receive state funding, membership is free. Forty Plus of New York, Inc. costs $399 with an additional $75 per month as long as one is an active member. Members of the New York chapter, which serves New Jersey and Connecticut, found positions with salaries of up to $150,000 within six months of joining, according to a spokesperson. Each member is asked to come in every day for generally the first 10 days upon joining to sharpen job-seeking skills. The new member then goes before a "job jury" of members, who critique his or her résumé in detail and suggest improvements.

COMPANIES THAT HIRE OLDER WORKERS

Some companies are noted for their innovative use of older workers. For example, Days Inns of America, the third-largest hotel chain in the United States, began hiring employees age 50 and over as reservations agents after experiencing high turnover with younger workers. A study of its Atlanta reservations system by the Commonwealth Fund, a non-profit foundation, found:

> Older workers remain on the job much longer than younger workers—an average of three years compared to one year. This translated into the following cost savings: an average of $618 in annual training and recruitment costs for an older worker versus $1,742 for a younger worker.

> Older workers were trained to operate complex computer equipment in the same time as younger workers—two weeks—after a half-day of familiarization.

> Older workers generated more revenue than younger workers. Although they took longer to handle each telephone call, they booked more reservations.

> Older workers worked all three shifts.

Many of the over 1,100 Days Inns hotels nationwide have also hired older workers, with gratifying results.

Other companies have also found older workers mean reliability, low turnover and absence rates, and punctuality. The Riese Organization, which owns and operates 187 fast-food and full-service restaurants in New York City—from the Pizza Hut, Kentucky Fried Chicken, and Roy Rogers franchises to Houlihan's and Friday's—has hired a dozen 50+ workers who possess computer and clerical skills to staff its corporate office in the past year alone. The workers are referred to the company by the New York City Department of the Aging and the New York State Department of Labor. "The seniors want their jobs, and that's the key," says James Ladota, vice president of human resources. "They are pleasant, punctual, and perform at least as well as younger workers."

The restaurant chain also plans to open a "mock" fast-food restaurant to train older workers in cashiering and food service skills in cooperation with the Department of the Aging later this year. "This restaurant will offer the opportunity to learn in a nonthreatening environment," says Mr. Ladota.

RÉSUMÉS

Dates of employment and graduation from college can be eliminated, as they pinpoint your age for the interviewer. At any rate, include no more than 20 years' experience, zeroing in on what is current and directly related to the job you are seeking. Only one or two pages, please—don't think three pages is necessary because you have 30 years of experience. Believe me, it's not all relevant, and will only annoy the interviewer. (See Chapter 2 for some résumés of older workers.)

JOB BANKS

Increasingly, employers are forming corporate job banks—or internal temporary pools—to fill their needs for trained temporary help for heavy workloads, special projects, and skills shortages. Dissatisfied with the cost and quality of temporary agency employees, they are finding retired workers—due to their familiarity with the company and its culture and their strong work ethic—a valuable source of labor.

A report by the Conference Board, "Job Banks for Retirees," describes some of these job banks:

The Travelers Corporation, mentioned earlier in this chapter, formed a job bank for retirees in 1981. Currently, over 700 retirees—about half ex-employees—are listed and on call for temporary assignments. While positions are mainly secretarial and clerical, some are for professionals. The job bank, which fulfills about 60% of The Travelers' needs for temporary help, saved the company $871,000 in temporary agency fees and sales tax in 1989, according to a Commonwealth Fund report.

Combustion Engineering, a Connecticut-based company, has about 400 people listed in its temporary employment program, of whom about 30%–40% are retirees. Spouses of retired workers can also join the pool, which offers jobs requiring technical or clerical skills.

Sovran Financial Corporation's Virginia-based temporary poll, On Call, Inc., formed in 1977, lists about 1,700 workers in Virginia, Maryland, Delaware, and Washington, DC. About 20% of the temporary workers in its biggest region are retirees. Teller, clerical, professional, and technical jobs are available.

Wells Fargo has about 650 retirees listed in its retirees-only job bank, 80% of whom have teller and clerical skills.

Los Angeles–based Aerospace Corporation, a nonprofit research firm which does studies for the U.S. Air Force Space Division, has a job bank with about 250 retirees. The focus is on engineering and technical skills, although some jobs are secretarial or clerical.

TEMPORARY AGENCIES

There are currently about 1.6 million temporary workers in the United States, according to the National Association of Temporary Services in Alexandria, Virginia. Increasingly, temporaries now include white-collar professionals—at all levels from middle-management to chief executive and chief financial officer positions—and technical workers, since so many companies are downsizing, restructuring, and doing special projects. Of the total annual payroll for temporary workers, 5.2% are "professionals" and 12% are "technical" workers. While there are no hard and fast statistics on how many temporaries ultimately are hired by the companies where they have temped, 38% of 2,100 temps surveyed were offered full-time jobs while on temporary assignment, notes the National Temporary Services Association.

Over 200 firms supply executive temps in the United States—a 400% increase over the past four years—according to the *Directory of Executive Temporary Placement Firms*. A notable firm in the field is IMCOR (Interim Management Corp.), which maintains a database of 15,000 candidates and places 200 temporary executives a year—of which 40% become permanent employees.

Many different fields represented by executive temporary placement firms are listed in the directory. To mention just a few: for law there are Special Counsel and Attorneys Per Diem; sales and marketing, C. Berger & Company and MB Inc.; finance and accounting, Account-Pros and Bankers On Call; health care, CanMed Consultants and The Nielsen Healthcare Group; publishing, Professional Assignments of New York; and engineering and manufacturing, ALTCO Temporary Services and TRS.

AGENCIES SPECIALIZING IN OLDER WORKERS

Among the more "traditional" temporary agencies, which handle predominantly secretarial and clerical positions, Kelly Services has a program for workers 55 and over for secretarial and clerical assignments called ENCORE. Formed in 1987, ENCORE operates in all Kelly offices in the United States and Canada.

Some temporary agencies have been formed which serve older workers exclusively. Retiree Skills, Inc., lists over 700 retirees and serves over 300 businesses in the Tucson, Arizona, area. Another temporary agency for older workers is Superior Senior Services Inc., which has over 300 older people listed for jobs in Minneapolis.

Operation ABLE is a nonprofit organization which helps workers 50 and over find jobs in the Chicago area. Its temporary employment service, APT, has listings for clerical jobs.

The Senior Career Planning and Placement Service, the New York–based executive search arm of the nonprofit National Executive Service Corps, places retired corporate executives in temporary assignments for mostly small and emerging companies on a national basis. A chief operating officer, who had previously earned $300,000, was placed in a position where he earned $100,000. The retired president of an Erie, Pennsylvania–based company, who earned over $100,000 annually, moved to Jamestown, New York, to become a vice president of operations for a furniture manufacturer. SCPPS also recruits executives for turnaround situations. For example, an interim president was placed for one year to improve manufacturing and marketing processes and downsize the company, notes David Willcox, managing director.

CHAPTER ELEVEN

Advice from Corporate Interviewers

Here's what corporate interviewers from a variety of industries, ranging from entertainment to banking to consumer products, say turns them on and off during interviews with job-seekers:

TALENT AGENCY

WILLIAM MORRIS AGENCY
PAT GALLOWAY, DIRECTOR OF HUMAN RESOURCES

DON'TS

"Gimmickry—I hate anything that's not businesslike. People should be able to stand on the basis of their own credentials," says Ms. Galloway, who directs recruiting for the famous trainee program of the world's biggest entertainment agency, where aspiring talent agents start in the mailroom at $300 per week. Legendary figures such as Michael Ovitz, David Geffen, and Barry Diller began their careers in the mailroom at William Morris, which has film, TV, book, theater, and commercials divisions. Résumés printed on T-shirts, stuffed in cans, Federal Expressed, or faxed, cover letters typed on stationery from a current employer, and used dirty sneakers—the job-seeker wanted to "get his foot in the door"—all fail to amuse Ms. Galloway, who prefers a professionally written letter with perfect spelling and grammar that gets to the point immediately.

More no-nos: "I've always been interested in entertainment" as a reason for wanting to be an agent—which ranks right up with "I'm a people person" in the hall of fame of vague, meaningless remarks for Ms. Galloway. People who are unable to discuss trends in the entertainment industry, are unfamiliar with its trade publications, such as *Variety* and *Hollywood Reporter* (or think *People* is a trade), and who seem caught up in the fantasy of the entertainment field are also undesirable. "We don't want any fanlike people here—the possibility of doing something uncool is too great. We want people to have a business perspective." Thank you notes on "teenage girlie stationery with lots of flowers or cats" are also out.

DO'S

Passion, sincerity, and focus. The ability to communicate clearly and succinctly is also essential, since "three-quarters of the job is on the phone." Career-changers are fine—some trainees in the agency's program, which takes five years and includes seminars, manuals, and constant observation of experienced agents, are former lawyers and business executives. Like anyone else, they must demonstrate a long-term interest in the field and a talent for sales. "I want the money I make to be tied to my performance," is a turn-on since it shows the applicant will be motivated to make money for the agency. Another good response: "I've always loved to sell talent, even as a kid." An "endearing, charming honesty" is a winner because it inspires trust.

HIGH-TECH

MICROSOFT CORPORATION
MICHELE GLASSER, RECRUITING MANAGER

DON'TS

Job-seekers without a sense of commitment and urgency for the high-tech field. A quick tip-off: people who do not incorporate technology into their daily lives, says Ms. Glasser, a recruiting manager at Microsoft, the leading computer software maker in the world with over 15,000 employees, whose software is used by over 180 million computers.

DO'S

Applicants who are "very bright—smart enough to face and solve problems they never imagined might be on their plates" and "very passionate about the software industry and how it will change the world." People who are analytical and creative, who "thrive on being inventive and thinking outside traditional boundaries"—according to a corporate brochure—are prized.

Interviewers probe to uncover the strategies behind applicants' accomplishments. Job-seekers who identify with the company and its mission to create the infrastructure that will drive PC technology for the next century are in demand. An ability to understand the fast-changing and flexible Microsoft culture, work independently, learn from one's mistakes, be results-oriented, and distinguish what is significant from what is not are key traits.

All this applies to entry-level positions as well. Microsoft hires an average of 200 employees through college recruitment efforts each year. "They get a very fast start, and there is a steep growth curve," Ms. Glasser notes.

TELEVISION

VIACOM
DWIGHT W. TIERNEY, VICE PRESIDENT AND CHAIRMAN, OFFICE OF THE EMPLOYEE ADVOCATE, VIACOM INC.

DON'TS

Job-seekers who want a job in TV but can't articulate why they want to work at MTV—where a survey of 3,000 employees found 93% either love or like working at the network—grate on Mr. Tierney, who directs hiring for high-middle to senior level positions. So do applicants who interrupt, avoid answering questions, or smoke—"too presumptuous and thoughtless."

DO'S

"Doing your homework" is something every interviewer applauds. However, for one woman who conducted an exploratory interview for a human resources job at Nickelodeon's production studios in Orlando, Florida, it paid off three years later. "She was incredibly well-informed about what we were doing and the kinds of people we were hiring, but no appropriate position was available," recalls Mr. Tierney. "So, when a spot came up at MTV Latino in Miami three years down the road—she was bilingual as well—we thought of her."

Questions popular in MTV interviews include: "What do you do with your leisure time? What books have you read lately? Who are you more like: your mother or your father? If you could change something in your life, what would it be?" Because MTV is a highly collegial environment where people from different divisions work on SWAT teams to problem-solve, it is important to gain insight into applicants' thinking processes to see whether they will be effective team players. "I try to find out who people are. If people like to spend their spare time reading, running, or hiking, chances are they like to be alone," says Mr. Tierney. "I'm not the standard interviewer."

Job-seekers who offer well-thought-out ideas—such as suggesting more animation or marketing ideas for VH1—do well, and some land consultant jobs at MTV.

ACCOUNTING

COOPERS & LYBRAND
BRENT C. INMAN, DIRECTOR OF NATIONAL RECRUITING

DON'TS

Defensiveness—"Talking about your deficiencies and making excuses, instead of spending time talking about your strengths."

DO'S

"We train our people not to recruit on first impressions—we have a systematic process and make decisions from the head, not the heart," says Mr. Inman of the college recruitment effort at Coopers & Lybrand, a "Big Six" accounting and consulting firm, which is the world's third-largest professional services firm with 95 offices in the United States. Bright people with judgment and commonsense, team players, and creative problem-solvers are sought after, while bilingual skills and a global perspective also rank high (25% of new hires this year can speak a second language).

A favored question to elicit self-assessment is "If you could do your college career over again, what would you do differently?" How the candidate handles the question and what it reveals are more important than the actual response, Mr. Inman notes. "The best indicator of future behavior is past behavior and results. We look at their record in terms of their entire life to date." On the other hand, "Tell me about yourself" is not used.

PUBLIC RELATIONS

BURSON-MARSTELLER
MARIA FORNARIO, SENIOR VICE PRESIDENT—
DIRECTOR OF HUMAN RESOURCES

DON'TS

"People who talk down to me because I'm in HR—who come across as too cocky," says Ms. Fornario. "I try to put them in their place." She adds: "I tend to be warm and open, and will ask lots of questions to get the information I need. This interview is not a power play." There are job-seekers who make it painfully obvious they have not done their homework, and think the company—the nation's biggest PR firm, with 1,000 employees in the United States and another 1,000 overseas—is an advertising agency. The ultimate turn-off: a job-seeker who enthused, "I'm so happy to be here at Hill & Knowlton," Burson-Marsteller's main competitor and the nation's second-largest PR agency.

Applicants who are too defensive, who disparage their former employers too much, and who are too chatty are also turn-offs, notes Ms. Fornario.

DO'S

"We look for people who offer a lot of value to our clients—who can help grow the business for the client and produce results for the client." As a result, a favorite interview question is: "What did you bring new and different to your current job?"

Prior experience in a public relations agency is not required—some employees come from government, corporations, or the nonprofit sector—but candidates should be aware an agency environment is very different. Juggling several accounts at one time, plus satisfying colleagues and clients, is required in shaping and communicating the proper message and image for clients. "We don't want people who think alike. We want people who can communicate in different ways, who will be very interested and involved in the industry, and want to make things happen."

Time management and the ability to work under pressure are important skills, since juggling projects and meeting deadlines is an agency fact of life, Ms. Fornario notes. Employees must continually realign their workload, deciding what can wait a bit and what must be done immediately, and ask for help if necessary.

CONSUMER PRODUCTS

COLGATE-PALMOLIVE
DANIEL J. FANOK, MANAGER OF STAFFING

DON'TS

"Candidates shoot themselves in the foot all the time—it's like that old Art Linkletter book *Kids Say the Darnedest Things*," says Mr. Fanok, who recruits primarily for the company's U.S. headquarters at all levels. Enthusiasm that verges on silliness is a case in point: "One candidate kept cracking jokes all the time—to the point where I felt like telling him to take a Valium and calm down. It was like interviewing Henny Youngman." Another job-seeker made the surprising confession that "I really don't know why I'm here—I wanted to get the recruiter off my back." Yet another betrayed a low energy level, admitting at 2:30 P.M. after an all-day round of interviews that she felt "really tired."

Another don't: coming to an interview unarmed—without questions. "There's nothing quite so puzzling to an interviewer as when a candidate has not a single question to ask." Or forcing an interviewer to "play 20 questions and practically beat the answers out of them. A good applicant will volunteer information and anticipate the question."

DO'S

While an overdose of enthusiasm is too much, the right amount is "the most important trait," says Mr. Fanok. "Basically, we look for three things when hiring—can he or she do it, or technical competence; is he or she willing to do it, or eagerness to do the hours, the job, the city; and can he or she fit into the corporate culture." The ability to demonstrate a "fact-benefit"—what a job-seeker has accomplished and how it will benefit the prospective employer—is also very important.

Candidates should be direct and to the point—no meandering, which wastes the interviewer's precious time—and able to sell ideas well. Being a team player is also crucial, since "it's increasingly rare for a person to go in like the Lone Ranger to clean up a town nowadays."

LAW

Jones Day Reavis Pogue
James Hagy, Chairman, Recruiting Committee

DON'TS

Only 10% of candidates in on-campus interviews for associate positions are prepared to answer why Jones Day Reavis Pogue is a good fit for them, notes Mr. Hagy, a partner in the Chicago office and chairman of the recruitment committee of the nation's second-largest law firm, with over 1,000 attorneys in 19 offices. The remainder seem to be unfamiliar with the firm, uninterested, lacking in energy, or shy. "Sometimes, in the first 30 seconds, you're already looking at your watch. You often get the thought they are sending résumés to 30–40 top law firms without noticing any differences between them," adds Mr. Hagy, whose firm receives 5,000–6,000 résumés a year.

Other no-no's: sounding overly ambitious by expressing a desire to become managing partner—Jones Day wants attorneys who are interested in client service, and not motivated primarily by money and status. Sending résumés without academic records—"people assume the worst. Always include them as part of your overall profile." One hapless job-seeker struck out by informing a surprised Mr. Hagy that he and his family "knew Jim Hagy very well."

DO'S

Asking incisive questions, demonstrating knowledge of Jones Day's expertise in the intellectual property area and its international client base, for example. "Those interviews fly by in a minute." Positive personality attributes make successful lawyers, and real life experience weighs in with class rankings at Jones Day: "We're looking for great people skills. Lawyers must also be amateur psychologists with the ability to satisfy other people's demands and work together. We aren't looking for people who will have a successful but isolated practice."

Display outside interests or volunteer work which show useful attributes. Mr. Hagy recalls that when he was hired by Jones Day 20 years ago, his hobby as an amateur magician impressed the recruiter—since it indicated he was comfortable dealing with groups of people and able to hold their interest for lengthy periods of time. Mr. Hagy is not swayed by references: "Since I never see references which say anything bad about a person, I seldom expect them to be the deciding factor."

ADVERTISING

GREY ADVERTISING
KEVIN BERGIN, SENIOR VICE PRESIDENT—
DIRECTOR OF HUMAN RESOURCES

DON'TS

Mouthing "I love commercials" is not the way to woo interviewers at Grey, the eighth-largest advertising agency in the world with 6,500 employees, including 2,000 in the United States—"they probably spend too much time in front of the TV," says Mr. Bergin. Another faux pas: outdated homework. Reading old reference materials and writing to people who have left the agency is counterproductive—always call to obtain current information, Mr. Bergin advises. And then there was the overconfident job-seeker who, when the interview was over, cheerily asked, "When do I start?"—temporarily stunning the interviewer.

DO'S

Entry-level job-seekers should show what they have done that demonstrates a passion for and interest in advertising—for example, internships at ad agencies, selling ads for the school newspaper, belonging to an advertising club, doing marketing for an organization, or volunteer work. An outgoing nature with excellent communication skills is desired. "Everyone's always presenting in advertising—all day long you're being challenged on how to position a product in the market so it will be successful. You have to be unafraid to articulate your opinions in a group."

"Give me a personal item you purchased recently and tell me why you purchased it" is a favorite question: the interviewer seeks to discover if the job-seeker has insight into his or her own consumer behavior.

PHARMACEUTICALS

Pfizer
Chuck Dombeck, Vice President—Employee Resources, U.S. Pharmaceuticals Group

DON'TS

"People who oversell themselves—there's a difficult balance between self-confidence, leadership, and arrogance," says Mr. Dombeck. This is particularly important because Pfizer, one of the nation's largest pharmaceutical companies with 25,000 employees worldwide, including 15,000 in the United States, has undergone a very significant shift to a flatter, less hierarchical structure with a greater emphasis on teamwork. "People need to be able to contribute their excellence to a team." On the other hand, being too passive is a negative—an applicant needs to strike a happy medium between being a good listener and passivity.

DO'S

Demonstrate an ability to be a team player by showing you have participated in and/or volunteered for cross-functional teams beyond your project area in your previous or current job. This is common at Pfizer—for example, an employee in finance may contribute his or her expertise to the medical processing area or to the marketing areas. In fact, line managers from different divisions are involved often in the interviewing process, which generally includes at least five people during a round of interviews.

Flexibility is another key trait, since the pharmaceuticals industry is changing so rapidly. Show you have moved across functional areas or held supervisory and nonsupervisory positions in another company.

"What is one question you did not want to be asked?" is a favorite of Mr. Dombeck, who says job-seekers are "amazingly open" in response to this effort to probe their weaknesses. Explanations of gaps in a résumé—or admissions that responsibilities on a project were overstated—are frequent, and Mr. Dombeck notes such candor only increases his esteem for the applicant.

BANKING

BANKERS TRUST
COLETTE GARDNER, VICE PRESIDENT, GLOBAL
MARKETS

DON'TS

No eye contact is a certain turn-off: "Forget it—I wouldn't trust the candidate. In the financial services industry, you can't take a risk like that," says Ms. Gardner, who recruits primarily for entry-level jobs in all financial services divisions at Bankers Trust, including sales and trading, corporate finance, capital markets, and client advisory services. Ditto for any misrepresentations on résumés: complete candor about periods of unemployment is preferred. Defensiveness is also a no-no.

While there's no right answer to one of Ms. Gardner's favorite self-assessment questions, "What would you like to change about yourself?" there is a definite wrong answer: "Nothing." Such a response indicates the candidate is arrogant, will be hard to manage, and most likely is not a team player. Some no-no's are real showstoppers—Ms. Gardner's all-time unforgettable answer to her question on why an applicant chose accounting as a major: "God directed me."

DO'S

Other questions which help the interviewer probe what motivates a job-seeker, like "Describe yourself in one word," "How would your peers describe you?" "What would you change about yourself?" and "What are you most proud of?" are popular. Again, no one answer will strike a "hot button" at Bankers Trust, one of the nation's largest banks (although one of the key traits listed in Chapter 5, such as integrity, leadership, flexibility, or an ability to work independently, is recommended). However, a deeply personal or family-oriented response to a question on what accomplishment a job-seeker takes most pride in will resonate with Ms. Gardner, she notes.

MAGAZINE PUBLISHING

HEARST
KENNETH FELDMAN, VICE PRESIDENT—
DIRECTOR, HUMAN RESOURCE S

DONT'S

"Verbal bombast," as well as interrupting the interviewer, fidgeting, and no eye contact. Job applications which do not match an applicant's résumé: "Are you or are you not who you were when you wrote to us?" asks Mr. Feldman, who is involved in and responsible for the recruitment process for most positions for Hearst Magazines, which includes women's service magazines like *Cosmopolitan* and *Good Housekeeping* and men's magazines like *Esquire* and *Popular Mechanics*. Top editors, he notes, are "celebrities who are handled at the top level of the Hearst Corporation," which is the largest privately held communications corporation in the world.

Some mistakes are more tragic than funny, says Mr. Feldman, such as job-seekers who talk about magazines that do not belong to the Hearst stable, such as *Vogue* or *Harper's* (*Harper's Bazaar*, however, is a Hearst publication), or who get the interviewer's name wrong. Another don't: job-hoppers who hopscotch every 9–18 months. "We prefer dedication, loyalty, and some stability."

DO'S

Well-prepared job-seekers who know about Hearst's wide variety of magazines, and have a good idea of where they can fit in and make a contribution—instead of just being starry-eyed about the magazine world and lacking focus. A well-rounded quality with a balance of work experience and community involvement or hobbies is highly desirable. "Half of what we look for is what they know—the other half is who they are."

Resources for the Job Hunt

The following listing of career trade associations, publications, and directories will be helpful in your job search. A list of computer databases and recommended books for business information and job-hunting is also included. Many publications and directories are also available on-line; check with your local library or with the on-line service to which you subscribe.

OCCUPATIONAL RESOURCES

ACCOUNTING

Publications

Accounting News
395 Hudson St.
New York, NY 10014
212-367-7652

Corporate Accounting
Lafferty Publications
420 Lexington Ave.
New York, NY 10170
212-557-6726

The CPA Journal
530 Fifth Ave.
New York, NY 10036
212-719-8300

The Journal of Accountancy
Harborside Financial Center
201 Plaza III
Jersey City, NJ 07311
201-938-3000

Management Accounting
Institute of Management Accountants
PO Box 433
Ten Paragon Drive
Montvale, NJ 07645
201-573-6275

Directories

Directory of Leading Accounting Firms World-Wide
12342 Northup Way
Bellevue, WA 98005
206-869-0655

ADVERTISING

American Association of Advertising Agencies
666 Third Ave.
New York, NY 10017
212-682-2500

American Advertising Federation
1400 K Street, NW
Washington, DC 20005
202-898-0089

Publications

Advertising Age
220 East 42nd St.
New York, NY 10017
212-210-0100

Adweek
1515 Broadway
New York, NY 10036
212-536-5336

Business Marketing
740 North Rush St.
Chicago, IL 60611
312-649-5260

Directories

AAAA Roster
American Association of Advertising Agencies
666 Third Ave.
New York, NY 10017
212-682-2500

Standard Directory of Advertising Agencies
121 Chanlon Road
New Providence, NJ 07974
908-464-6800

BANKING/FINANCE

American Bankers Association
1120 Connecticut Ave., NW
Washington, DC 20036
202-663-5000

Bank Administration Institute
One North Franklin St.
Chicago, IL 60606
312-553-4600

Financial Executives Institute
PO Box 1938
Ten Madison Avenue
Morristown, NJ 07962
973-898-4600

Financial Managers Society
230 W. Monroe St.
Chicago, IL 60606
312-578-1300

Financial Women International
200 N. Glebe Road
Arlington, VA 22203
703-807-2007

Financial Women's Association of New York
215 Park Avenue South
New York, NY 10003
212-533-2141

Mortgage Bankers Association of America
1125 15th St., NW
Washington, DC 20005
202-861-6500

National Association of Urban Bankers
1010 Wayne Ave.
Silver Spring, MD 20910
301-589-2141

Publications

ABA Banking Journal
Simmons-Boarman Publishing Corp.
345 Hudson St.
New York, NY 10014
212-620-7200

American Banker
One State Street Plaza
New York, NY 10004
212-803-6700

Bankers Magazine
395 Hudson St.
New York, NY 10014
212-367-7652

The Bond Buyer
One State Street Plaza
New York, NY 10004
212-803-6700

CFO (Chief Financial Officer)
253 Summer St.
Boston, MA 02210
617-345-9700

Global Finance
1001 Avenue of the Americas
New York, NY 10018
212-768-1100

Institutional Investor
488 Madison Ave.
New York, NY 10022
212-224-3300

Journal of Commercial Lending
Robert Morris Associates
One Liberty Place
1650 Market St.
Philadelphia, PA 19107
215-851-9100

United States Banker
11 Penn Plaza
New York, NY 10001
212-967-7000

Directories

American Bank Directory
4709 West Golf Road
Skokie, IL 60076
800-321-3373

American Banker Yearbook
One State Street Plaza
New York, NY 10004
212-803-6700

Corporate Finance Sourcebook
121 Chanlon Road
New Providence, NJ 07974
800-521-8110

Moody's Bank and Finance Manual
Moody's Investor Service, Inc.
99 Church St.
New York, NY 10007
212-553-0300

Who's Who in Credit and Financial Management
New York Credit and Financial Management Association
49 W. 45th St.
New York, NY 10036
212-944-2400

Who's Who in Finance and Industry
121 Chanlon Road
New Providence, NJ 07974
800-521-8110

BROADCASTING

American Women in Radio and Television
1650 Tysons Blvd.
McLean, VA 22102
703-506-3290

Academy of Television Arts and Sciences
5220 Lankershim Blvd.
North Hollywood, CA 91601
818-754-2800

International Radio and Television Society
420 Lexington Ave.
New York, NY 10170
212-867-6650

National Association of Broadcasters
1771 N St., NW
Washington, DC 20036
202-429-5300

National Cable Television Association
1724 Massachusetts Ave., NW
Washington, DC 20036
202-775-3550

Radio Advertising Bureau
261 Madison Ave.
New York, NY 10016
212-681-7200

Radio-Television News Directors Association
1000 Connecticut Ave., NW
Washington, DC 20036
202-659-6510

Television Bureau of Advertising
850 Third Ave.
New York, NY 10022
212-486-1111

Publications

Broadcasting & Cable
1705 DeSales St., NW
Washington, DC 20036
202-659-2340

Daily Variety
5700 Wilshire Blvd.
Los Angeles, CA 90036
213-857-6600

Electronic Media
740 North Rush St.
Chicago, IL 60611
312-649-5293

Variety
249 W. 17th St.
New York, NY 10011
212-323-4345

ENGINEERING

American Association of Engineering Societies
1111 19th Street, NW
Washington , DC 20036
202-296-2237

American Institute of Aeronautics and Astronautics
Aerospace Center
370 L'Enfant Promenade, SW
Washington, DC 20024
202-646-7400

American Institute of Chemical Engineers
345 East 47th Street
New York, NY 10017
212-705-7338

Institute of Electrical and Electronics Engineers
345 East 47th Street
New York, NY 10017
212-705-7900

Institute of Industrial Engineers
25 Technology Park/Atlanta
Norcross, GA 30092
404-449-0460

National Society of Professional Engineers
1420 King Street
Alexandria, VA 22314
703-684-2800

Society of Women Engineers
120 Wall Street
New York, NY 10005
212-509-9577

Publications

ENR (Engineering News-Record)
McGraw-Hill, Inc.
PO Box 516
Hightstown, NJ 08520
800-525-5003

IEEE Engineering Management Review
445 Hoes Lane
Box 1331
Piscataway, NJ 08855
732-562-3800

IEEE Spectrum
345 E. 47th St.
New York, NY 10017
212-705-7900

HEALTH CARE

American College of Healthcare Executives
1 N. Franklin
Chicago, IL 60606
312-424-2800

American Dental Association
211 E. Chicago Ave.
Chicago, IL 60611
312-440-2736

American Nurses Association
600 Maryland Ave., SW
Washington, DC 20024
202-554-4444

American Pharmaceutical Association
2215 Constitution Ave., NW
Washington, DC 20037
202-628-4410

American Physical Therapy Association
1111 N. Fairfax St.
Alexandria, VA 22314
800-999-2782

American Public Health Association
1015 15th St., NW
Washington, DC 20005
202-789-5600

National Association of Social Workers
750 First St. NE
Washington, DC 20002
800-638-8799

Publications

American Journal of Hospital Pharmacy
7272 Wisconsin Ave.
Bethesda, MD 20814
301-657-3000

American Journal of Nursing
555 W. 57th St.
New York, NY 10019
212-582-8820

Hospitals & Health Networks
737 N. Michigan Ave.
Chicago, IL 60611
312-440-6800

Journal of the American Dental Association
211 E. Chicago Ave.
Chicago, IL 60611
312-440-2736

Journal of the American Medical Association
515 N. State St.
Chicago, IL 60610
312-464-4512

NASW News
750 First St. NE
Washington, DC 20002
800-638-8799

RN
5 Paragon Drive
Montvale, NJ 07645
201-358-7200

Directories

Hospital Phone Book
121 Chanlon Road
New Providence, NJ 07974
800-521-8110

HIGH-TECH

Association for Computing Machinery
1515 Broadway
New York, NY 10036
212-869-7440

Computer & Communications Industry Association
666 11th St., NW
Washington, DC 20001
202-783-0070

Electronics Industries Association
2500 Wilson Blvd.
Arlington, VA 22201
703-907-7500

IEEE Computer Society
1730 Massachusetts Avenue, NW
Washington, DC 20036
202-371-0101

Information Industry Association
555 New Jersey Ave., NW
Washington, DC 20001
202-986-0280

Information Technology Association of America
1616 N. Ft. Myer Drive, Suite 1300
Arlington, VA 22209
703-522-5055

Society for Information Management
401 North Michigan Avenue
Chicago, IL 60611
312-644-6610

Publications

Computerworld
500 Old Connecticut Path
Framingham, MA 01701
508-879-0700

Industry Standard (Internet trends)
315 Pacific Avenue
San Francisco, CA 94111
415-733-5400

Internet World
Mecklermedia
20 Ketchum St.
Westport, CT 06880
203-226-6967

Journal of Management Information Systems
80 Business Park Drive
Armonk, NY 10504
914-273-1800

PC Computing
50 Beale St.
San Francisco, CA 94105
415-578-7000

PC World
501 Second St.
San Francisco, CA 94107
415-243-0500

UPSIDE (Internet trends)
2015 Pioneer Court
San Mateo, CA 94403
888-998-7743

Directories

Computer Industry Almanac
The Reference Press
6448 Highway 290 E.
Austin, TX 78723
800-486-8666

Hoover's Guide to Computer Companies
The Reference Press
6448 Highway 290 E.
Austin, TX 78723
800-486-8666

MAGAZINE PUBLISHING

American Society of Magazine Editors
919 Third Ave.
New York, NY 10022
212-752-0055

Magazine Publishers of America
919 Third Ave.
New York, NY 10022
212-872-3700

Publications

Folio: The Magazine for Magazine Management
11 Riverbend Drive South
PO Box 4272
Stamford, CT 06907
203-358-9900

Directories

Bacon's Publicity Checker: Periodicals
Bacon's Publishing Company
332 South Michigan
Chicago, IL 60604
312-922-2400

Burrelle's Media Directory
75 East Northfield Road
Livingston, NJ 07039
973-992-6600

Standard Rate and Data Service:
Business Publication Rates and Data
1700 Higgins Road
Des Plaines, IL 60018
847-375-5000

MANUFACTURING

National Association of Manufacturers
1331 Pennsylvania Avenue NW
Washington, DC 20004
202-637-3000

Society of Manufacturing Engineers
P.O. Box 930
1 SME Drive
Dearborn, MI 48121
313-271-1500

Publications

Electronic Manufacturing News
Cahners Publishing
275 Washington Street
Newton, MA 02158
617-964-3030

Manufacturing Engineering
Society of Manufacturing Engineers
P.O. Box 920
1 SME Drive
Dearborn, MI 48121
313-271-1500

Manufacturing Today
Cahners Publishing
275 Washington Streer
New ton, MA 02158
617-964-3030

Directories

Harris Infosource (by state or region)
2057 E. Aurora Road
Twinsburg, OH 44087
800-888-5900

Manufacturers Register
1633 Central St.
Evanston, IL 60201
847-864-7000

Moody's Industrial Manual
Moody's Investors Service
99 Church St.
New York, NY 10007
212-553-0300

Thomas Register of American Manufacturers (by product)
Thomas Publishing Co.
1 Penn Plaza
New York, NY 10119
212-290-7200

PUBLIC RELATIONS

Public Relations Society of America
33 Irving Place
New York, NY 10003
212-995-2230

Women in Communications
2101 Wilson Boulevard
Arlington, VA 22201
703-528-4200

Publications

O'Dwyer's Newsletter
J. R. O'Dwyer Co., Inc.
271 Madison Avenue
New York, NY 10016
212-679-2471

Public Relations Journal
33 Irving Place
New York, NY 10003
212-995-2230

Public Relations Quarterly
44 West Market Street
P.O. Box 311
Rhinebeck, NY 12572
914-876-2081`

Directories

O'Dwyer's Directory of Corporate Communications
J. R. O'Dwyer Co., Inc.
271 Madison Avenue
New York, NY 10016
212-679-2471

O'Dwyer's Directory of Public Relations Firms
J. R. O'Dwyer Co., Inc.
271 Madison Avenue
New York, NY 10016
212-679-2471

PUBLISHING (BOOKS)

Association of American Publishers
71 Fifth Ave.
New York, NY 10003
212-255-0200

Women's National Book Association
160 Fifth Ave.
New York, NY 10010
212-675-7805

Publications

Publisher's Weekly
249 W. 17th St.
New York, NY 10011
800-278-2991

Directories

Publishers Directory
Gale Research Company
835 Penobscot Building
Detroit, MI 48226
800-877-GALE

Literary Marketplace
121 Chanlon Road
New Providence, NJ 07974
800-521-8110

PURCHASING

National Association of Purchasing Management
2055 East Centennial Circle
Box 22160
Tempe, AZ 85285
800-888-6276

Publications

Purchasing
275 Washington St.
Newton, MA 02158
617-964-3030

Purchasing Today
2055 East Centennial Circle
Box 22160
Tempe, AZ 85285
800-888-6276

Directories

(Refer to general business directories -- *Dun's Million Dollar Directory, Thomas Register of American Manufacturers, Moody's Industrial Manual* -- etc.)

REAL ESTATE/CONSTRUCTION

American Building Contractors Association
Box 39277
Downey, CA 90239
714-828-4760

Building Owners and Managers Association International
1201 New York Ave. NE
Washington, DC 20005
202-408-2662

International Development Research Council (corporate real estate)
35 Technology Parkway
Norcross, GA 30092
770-446-8955

National Association of Home Builders
1201 15th St., NW
Washington, DC 20005
202-822-0200

Publications

The Builder
Hanley-Wood
1 Thomas Circle
Washington, DC 20005
202-452-0800

ENR
1221 Avenue of the Americas
New York, NY 10020
212-512-6428

National Real Estate Investor
9800 Metcalf
Overland Park, KS 66202
770-955-2500

Real Estate Forum
111 Eighth Ave.
New York, NY 10011
212-563-6460

Real Estate Weekly
One Madison Ave.
New York, NY 10010
212-679-1234
770-446-8955

Directories

U.S. Real Estate Register
Barry, Inc.
Box 551
Wilmington, MA 01887
800-752-1269

RETAILING

National Retail Federation
325 7th St. NW
Washington, DC 20004
202-783-7971

Publications

Chain Store Age Executive
Lebhar-Friedman
425 Park Ave.
New York, NY 10022
212-756-5135

Stores
National Retail Federation Enterprises
325 7th St. NW
Washington, DC 20004
202-783-7971

Directories

Directory of Department Stores
3922 Coconut Palm Drive
Tampa, FL 33619
813-664-6700

Fairchild's Retail Stores Financial Directory
Fairchild Publications
7 W. 34th St.
New York, NY 10001
800-252-9764

SALES AND MARKETING

American Marketing Association
250 South Wacker Drive
Chicago, IL 60606
312-648-0536

International Marketing Institute
314 Hammond Street
Chestnut Hill, MA 02167
617-552-8690

Sales and Marketing Executives International
Statler Office Tower
Cleveland, OH 44115
216-771-6650

Publications

Business Marketing
Crane Communications
740 North Rush Street
Chicago, IL 60601
312-649-5260

Journal of Marketing
American Marketing Association
250 South Wacker Drive
Chicago, IL 60606
312-648-0536

Marketing News
American Marketing Association
250 South Wacker Drive
Chicago, IL 60606
312-648-0536

Sales and Marketing Management
355 Park Avenue South
New York, NY 10010
212-592-6300

Directories

Manufacturers' Agents National Association
Directory of Manufacturers' Sales Agencies
Box 3467
Laguna Hills, CA 92654
714-859-4040

Marketing and Sales Career Directory
Gale Research Company
835 Penobscot Building
Detroit, MI 48226
800-877-GALE

GENERAL RESOURCES

Associations

American Business Women's Association
PO Box 8728
9100 Ward Parkway
Kansas City, MO 64114
816-361-6621

American Management Association
1601 Broadway
New York, NY 10019
212-586-8100

Association of MBA Executives
5 Summit Pl.
Branford, CT 06405
203-315-5221

Catalyst
120 Wall St.
New York, NY 10005
212-514-7600

Forty-Plus Clubs
(nonprofit organization with many chapters across the country;
look in telephone directories or check with libraries)

National Association for Female Executives
30 Irving Place
New York, NY 10003
212-477-2200

National Management Association
2210 Arbor Boulevard
Dayton, OH 45439
937-294-0421

Publications

Barron's
200 Liberty Street, Tower A
New York, NY 10281
212-416-2700

Black Enterprise
130 Fifth Ave.
New York, NY 10011
212-242-8000

Business Week
1221 Avenue of the Americas
New York, NY 10020
212-512-2511

Crain Communications
(*Crain's Chicago Business, Cleveland Business, Detroit Business,
New York Business*, plus trade publications)
740 North Rush St.
Chicago, IL 60611
800-678-9595

Executive Female
30 Irving Place
New York, NY 10003
212-477-2200

Fast Company
77 N. Washington St.
Boston, MA 02114
617-937-0300

Forbes
60 Fifth Ave.
New York, NY   10011
212-620-2200

Fortune
1271 Avenue of the Americas
New York, NY 10020
212-586-1212

Inc.
38 Commercial Wharf
Boston, MA 02110
617-248-8000

National Business Employment Weekly
200 Liberty St., Tower A
New York, NY 10281
212-416-2000

Wall Street Journal
200 Liberty St., Tower A
New York, NY 10281
212-416-2000

Working Woman
135 W. 50th St.
New York, NY 10020
212-445-6100

Directories

Career Employment Opportunities Directory
Ready Reference Press
Box 5169
Santa Monica, CA 90405
213-474-5175

Corporate Yellow Book: Who's Who at Leading U.S. Companies
104 Fifth Avenue
New York, NY 10011
212-627-4140

Directory of Business Information Resources
Pocket Knife Square
Box 1866
Lakeville, CT 06039
203-435-0868

Directory of Corporate Affiliations
121 Chanlon Road
New Providence, NJ 07974
908-464-6800

Directories in Print
Gale Research Company
835 Penobscot Building
Detroit, MI 48226
800-877-GALE

Directory of Executive Temporary Placement Firms
Templeton Road
Fitzwilliam, NH 03447
603-585-6544

Directory of Executive Recruiters
Templeton Road
Fitzwilliam, NH 03447
603-585-6544

Dun's Business Rankings
3 Sylvan Way
Parsippany, NJ 07054
800-526-0651

Dun's Career Guide
3 Sylvan Way
Parsippany, NJ 07054
800-526-0651

Dun's Directory of Service Companies
3 Sylvan Way
Parsippany, NJ 07054
800-526-0651

Dun's Million Dollar Directory
3 Sylvan Way
Parsippany, NJ 07054
800-526-0651

Dun's Top 50,000 Companies
3 Sylvan Way
Parsippany, NJ 07054
800-526-0651

Dun's Reference Book of Corporate Managements
3 Sylvan Way
Parsippany, NJ 07054
800-526-0651

Encyclopedia of Associations
Gale Research Company
835 Penobscot Building
Detroit, MI 48226
800-877-GALE

Encyclopedia of Business Information Sources
Gale Research Company
835 Penobscot Building
Detroit, MI 48226
800-877-GALE

Guide to American Directories
Box 8503
Coral Springs, FL 33075
305-752-1708

Hoover's Handbook of American Business
The Reference Press
6448 Highway 290 E.
Austin, TX 78723
800-486-8666

Moody's Industrial Manual
Moody's Investor Service
99 Church Street
New York, NY 10007
212-553-0300

Standard & Poor's Register of Corporations, Directors and Executives
25 Broadway
New York, NY 10004
212-208-8283

Standard Directory of Advertisers
National Register Publishing
121 Chanlon Road
New Providence, NJ 07974
908-464-6800

Thomas Register of American Manufacturers
Thomas Publishing Company
5 Pennsylvania Plaza
New York, NY 10001
212-695-0500

Ward's Business Directory of U.S. Private and Pulbic Companies
Gale Research Company
835 Penobscot Building
Detroit, MI 48226
800-877-GALE

Who's Who in Finance and Industry
121 Chanlon Road
New Providence, NJ 07974
908-464-6800

Who's Who in the East, Midwest, South, etc.
121 Chanlon Road
New Providence, NJ 07974
908-464-6800

Mailing List Directories

Direct Marketing List Source
3004 Glenview Road
Wilmette, IL 60091
800-851-SRDS

The List Directory
Walter Karl Cos.
135 Bedford Road
Armonk, NY 10504
800-394-0294

Mailing Lists Directory
American Business Directories
5711 South 86th Circle
Omaha, NE 68127
402-593-4600

Computer Databases

Information on companies and abstracts of articles from business
publications:

ABI/INFORM
UMI
300 W. Zeeb Road
Box 1346
Ann Arbor, MI 48106
800-521-0600

Disclosure SEC Database
5161 River Road
Bethesda, MD 20816
800-754-9690

Dun's Business Records Plus
Marquis One Tower
245 Peachtree Center Ave.
Atlanta, GA 30303
800-235-4008

Dun's Global Families Online
Three Sylvan Way
Parsippany, NJ 07054
800-223-1026

Management Contents
Information Access Company
362 Lakeside Drive
Foster City, CA 94404
800-227-8431

Moody's Corporate News
Moody's Investor Services
99 Church St.
New York, NY 10007
800-342-5647

Moody's Corporate Profiles
Moody's Investor Services
99 Church St.
New York, NY 10007
800-342-5647

Predicasts F&F Index United States
Information Access Company
362 Lakeside Ave.
Foster City, CA 94404
800-321-6388

Standard & Poor's Corporate Descriptions
25 Broadway
New York, NY 10004
212-208-8300

Trade & Industry ASAP
Information Access Company
362 Lakeside Drive
Foster City, CA 94404
800-227-8431

Job Hunting Web Sites

Career Mosaic
http://www.careermosaic.com

Career Path
http://www.careerpath.com

E-Span
http://www.espan.com

FedWorld
http://www.fedworld.gov

JOBTRAK
http://www.jobtrak.com

MedSearch
http://www.medsearch.com

Monster Board
http://www.monster.com

Nonprofit Career Network
http://www.nonprofitcareer.com

Online Career Center
http://www.occ.com

Wall Street Journal Interactive's Careers
http://careers.wsj

Database and Information Broker Directories

Burwell Directory of Information Brokers
Burwell Enterprises
3724 FM 1960 W.
Houston, TX 77068
713-537-9051

Directory of Databases
Gale Research Company
835 Penobscot Building
Detroit, MI 48226
800-877-GALE

RECOMMENDED READING

Bernstein, Alan B. and Schaffzin, Nicholas R. *Guide to Your Career.* New York: Princeton Review, 1996.

Bloch, Deborah. *How to Have a Winning Job Interview (Here's How).* Lincolnwood, IL: NTC Contemporary, 1998.

Bloch, Deborah. *How to Write a Winning Resume.* Lincolnwood, IL: NTC Contemporary, 1993.

Bolles, Richard Nelson. *What Color Is Your Parachute?* Berkeley, CA: Ten Speed Press, 1998.

Caple, John. *The Ultimate Interview.* New York: Main Street Books, 1991.

Dixon, Pam. *Job Searching Online for Dummies.* Indianapolis: IDG Books, 1998.

Dorio, Marc. *The Complete Idiot's Guide to Getting the Job You Want.* New York: Macmillan/Alpha, 1995.

Eyler, David R. *Resumes That Mean Business.* New York: Random House, 1996.

Faux, Marion. *The Complete Resume Guide.* New York: Macmillan, 1995.

Glaser, Connie Brown and Smalley, Barbara Steinberg. *More Power to You! How Women Can Communicate the Way to Success.* New York: Warner Books, 1995.

Haft, Tim, Heenehan, Meg et al. *Job Smart: What You Need to Know to Get the Job You Want.* New York: Princeton Review, 1997.

Half, Robert. *How to Get a Better Job in This Crazy World.* New York: Signet, 1994.

Jackson, Tom and Jackson, Ellen. *The New Perfect Resume.* New York: Main Street Books, 1996.

Kennedy, Joyce Lain and Morrow, Thomas J. *The Electronic Job Search Revolution.* New York: John Wiley, 1995.

Medley, H. Anthony. *Sweaty Palms: The Neglected Art of Being Interviewed.* Berkeley, CA: Ten Speed Press, 1992.

Messmer, Max. *Job Hunting for Dummies.* Indianapolis: IDG Books, 1995.

Oldman, Mark and Hamadeh, Samer. *The Internship Bible.* New York: Princeton Review, 1995.

Parker, Yana. *The Damn Good Resume Guide.* Berkeley, CA: Ten Speed Press, 1996.

Petras, Kathryn and Ross. *The Only Job Hunting Guide You'll Ever Need.* New York: Poseidon Press, 1995.

Reed, Jean and Potter, Ray. *Resumes That Get Jobs.* New York: Macmillan/ARCO, 1998.

Wendleton, Kate. *Job-Search Secrets.* New York: Five O'Clock Books, 1997.

Wendleton, Kate. *Targeting the Job You Want.* New York: Five O'Clock Books, 1997.

Wynett, Stanley. *Cover Letters That Will Get You the Job You Want.* Cincinnati: Better Way Books, 1993.

Yate, Martin. Knock 'Em Dead: *The Ultimate Job Seeker's Handbook.* Holbrook, MA: Adams Media, 1998.